ABANDONED UPSTATE NEW YORK

NICHOLAS LONG

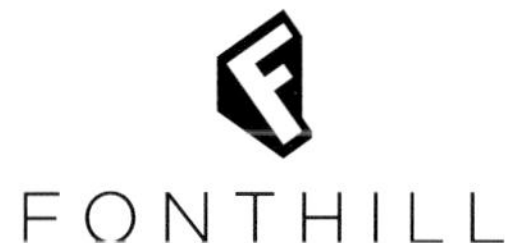

Fonthill Media Inc.
www.fonthillmedia.com
office@fonthillmedia.com

First published 2020

ISBN 978-1-63499-222-0

Typeset in Trade Gothic 10pt on 15pt
Printed and bound in England

CONTENTS

ABOUT THE AUTHOR

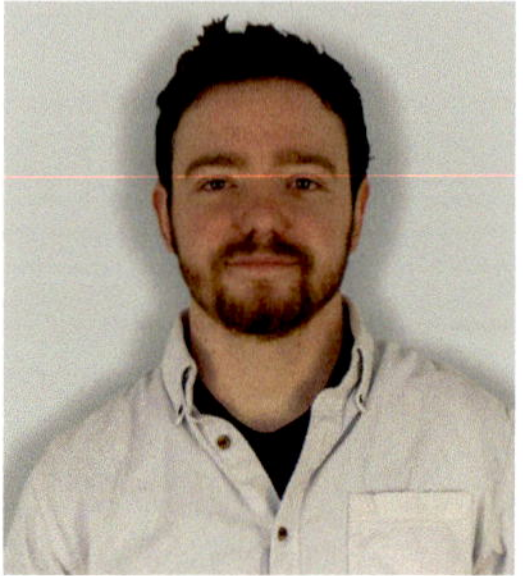

Nicholas Long has been hooked on abandoned photography ever since the day he accompanied his brother on a trip to an old abandoned food factory. Exploring the desolate remains of the past, mixed with the thrill of venturing into forgotten territory, rapidly grew into an addiction. With each location, a new vicarious experience of life lay before him. Nick became infatuated with researching each location he explored. He utilizes his photography and research as a means of keeping record of his experiences within each deserted find, serving as reminders of how far we have come in technological advances as a human race.

INTRODUCTION

Upstate New York has always been home to vast rural environments. It nourished strong agricultural production while providing opportunity to farmers and business entrepreneurs across the state. With the progression of time, urban renewal, and technology, many businesses and farms were forced to close or move, giving Mother Nature freedom to dispose of their memories as she saw fit. These memories, which lie under decades of debris, patiently wait for guests to revive them and tell their stories. Souvenirs, in the form of farmhouses, dairy factories, and mills, serve only as a glimpse of what life was like in Upstate New York.

Decaying buildings scar the landscape as they face demolition or repurposing. Some of these buildings or eyesores are quickly removed. But removing old factories and houses produces many risks to the teams hired to tear them down, and to the environment, such as black mold, asbestos exposure, and injury. Some of these locations stayed hidden from the public eye, prolonging their lifespan for explorers and, unfortunately, vandals, to view. These hidden gems tend to be less tampered with and a more invigorating experience, making the risks ever more rewarding. With the giants that I was extremely fortunate to explore, meticulous self-care went into every photo opportunity.

My photography passion began in 2016, as I was a premature photographer, naive to what experiences lay ahead of me on these intriguing endeavors. Like many early photographers do when they get their first camera, I was taking photos of absolutely everything: landscapes, animals, people, and nature. When I came to my first abandoned location, I found myself completely captivated by my surroundings, taking particularly small amounts of photos here and there. I became overwhelmed, taking in all the history and held great admiration for the beautiful clash between nature and past civilization. I knew this would only be the beginning of a new and rewarding pursuit.

I had become consumed with exploring new places and uncovering these lost memories scattered across Upstate New York. I was constantly on the lookout during my commutes to and from work and college. With much planning and preparation, I began exploring numerous houses that were sleeping on the roadside, as well as decrepit grocery stores and crumbling concrete mills. My confidence and excitement were growing, as well as my experience. Each location became more captivating and rewarding with rich history and information. I also began to make mental notes of the numerous dangers that were associated with my explorations, such as encountering homeless people, avoiding agitated drug addicts, stepping through floor boards, asbestos, mold, and the need to wear the proper clothing: a respirator, boots, and gloves. Many people would never consider putting themselves in any of the situations I have been in, and I fully understand. But I am not most people. I thrive on adventure, and the thrill of exploration.

With my first book, I wish for you to see and experience Upstate New York in all her beauty, mystery, and vulnerability, and I hope you are left feeling a tantalizing need to see and learn more. Until my next series of adventures, enjoy!

1

ABBASS FOOD CORPORATION

1966-2004

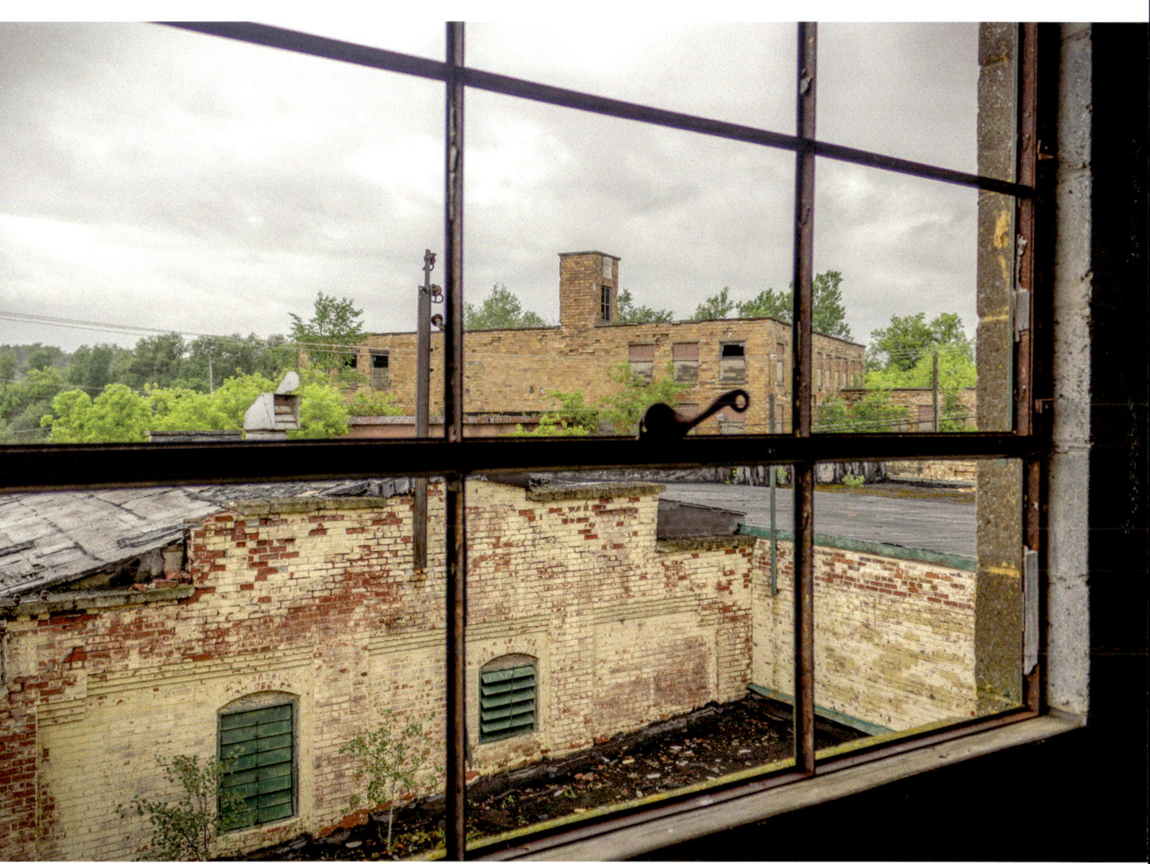

Originally started by two brothers in the early 1950s, the Abbass Food Corporation became active in the neighboring town of Carthage, NY. In the mid-1960s, the corporation relocated to its final resting place in Evans Mills, NY. The Abbass Food Corporation would continue to run for almost forty years before becoming inactive in 2004.

This factory was the first location I had ever explored and set the bar high for my future expectations. Walking into the primary assembly room, on the ground level, and experiencing nothing but total darkness and the faint echo of crickets was quite an adrenaline rush. As my eyes began to adjust, I pulled out my camera and flashlight, to venture deeper into the factory. Each room was engulfed in tremendous amounts of debris and remnants of the corporation. Making my way through the countless corridors and vandalized rooms, I came to a large hole in the wall. I crawled through and discovered a deep underground tunnel. With flashlight in hand, I crawled deeper and deeper down this tunnel and found a new environment, hidden from the light of day. This historical place left its grip on me, which gave me the desire to make many additional trips back.

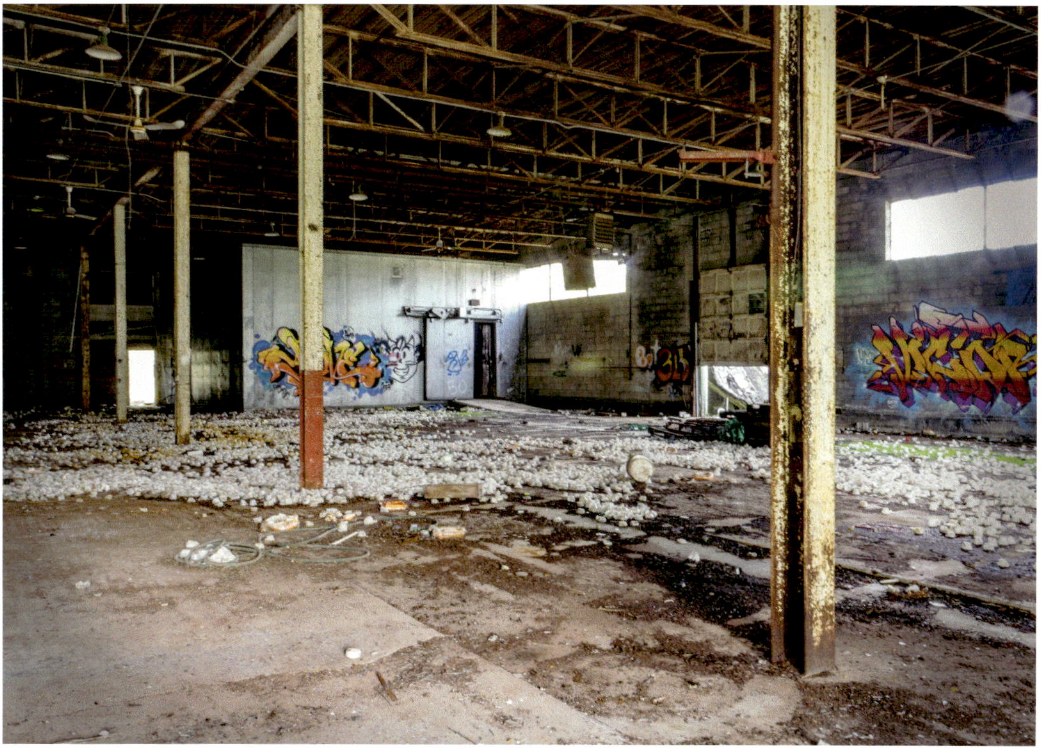

Primary assembly room, littered with plastic milk cups left by the corporation.

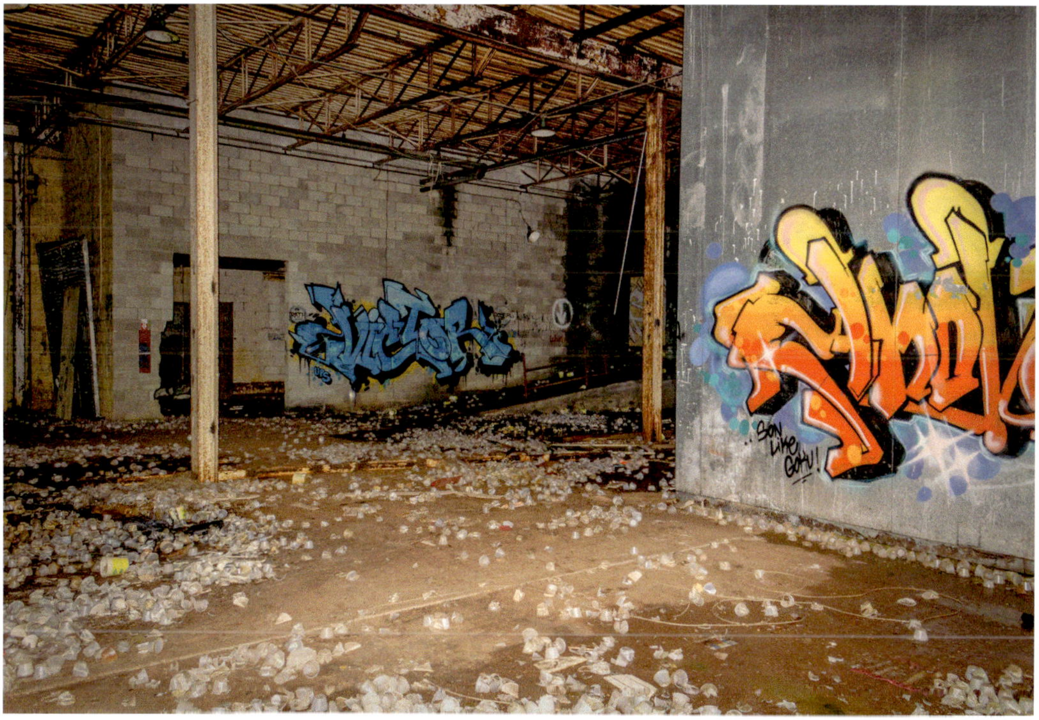

Standing to the left of the freezer room, viewing the primary assembly room from another angle.

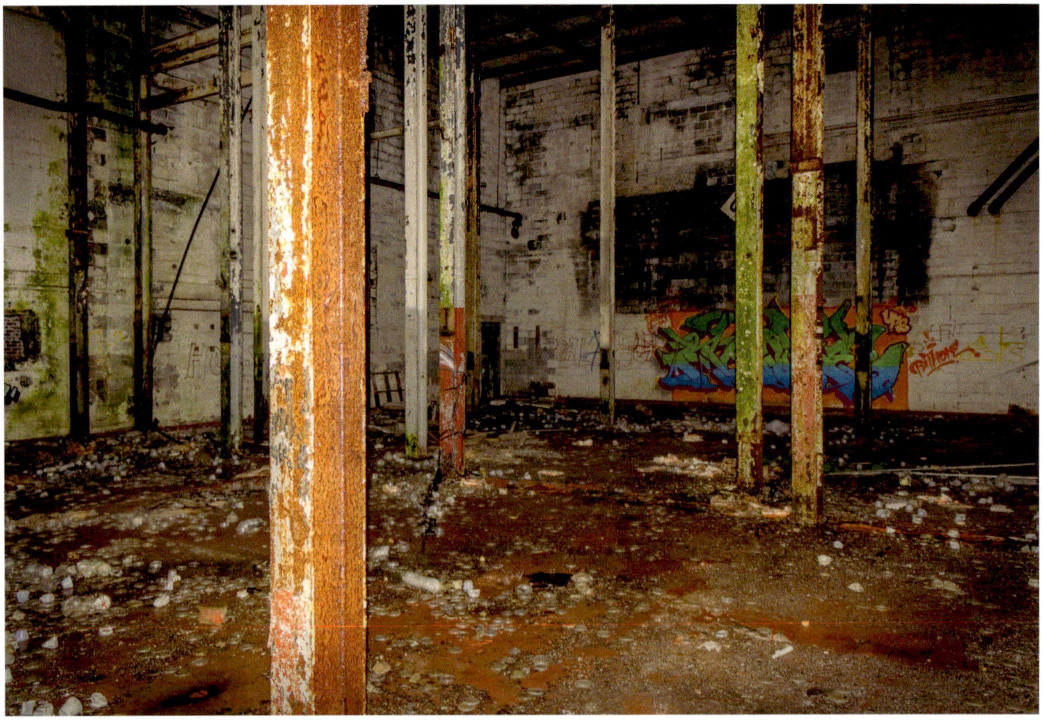

Secondary assembly room, supported by withering steel beams and dressed in graffiti.

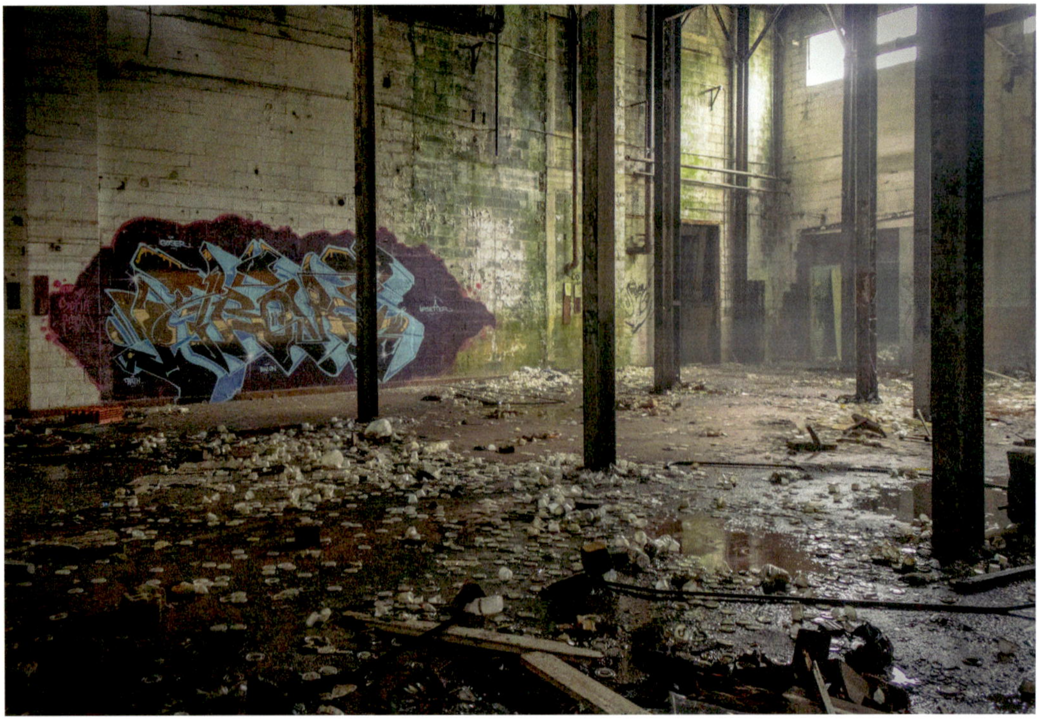

Another glimpse of the secondary assembly room, soaked in run-off water from the third floor.

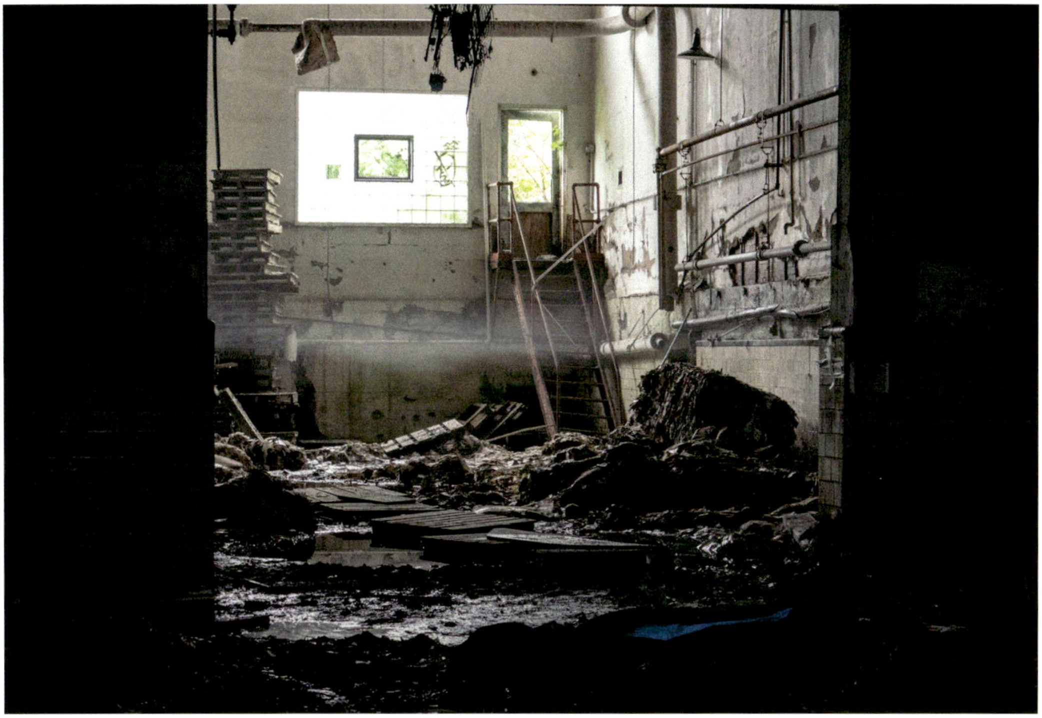

An entrance into what appears to be a storage section of the facility, flooded in murky water, blanketed in a sheet of fog.

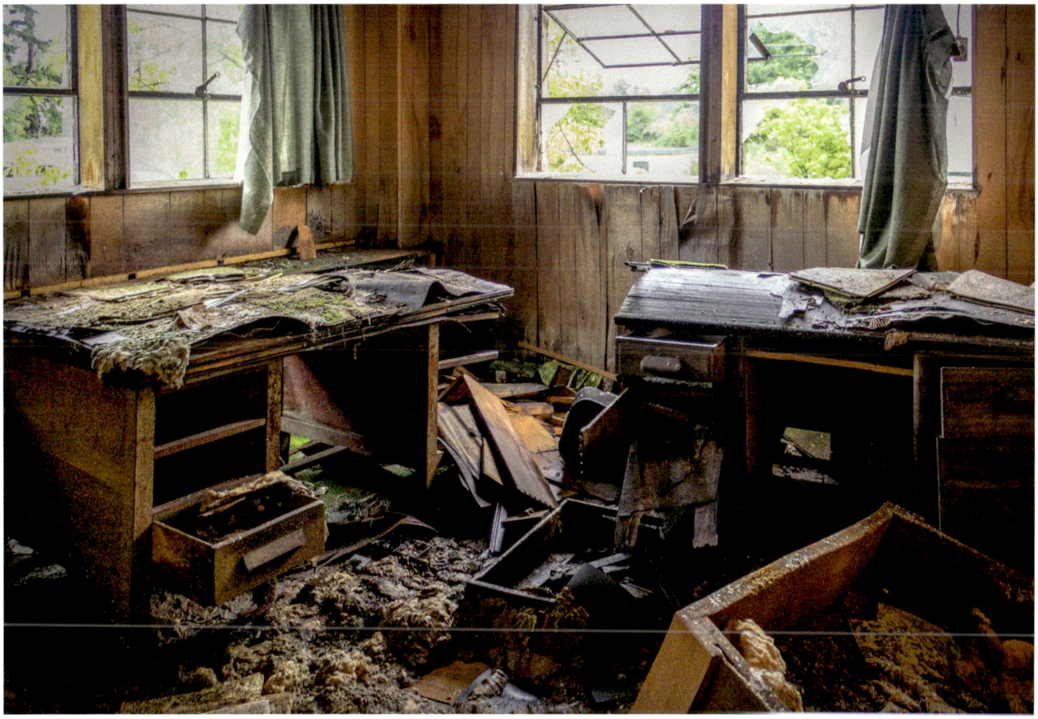

A section of the corporate offices, heavily deteriorated and covered in insulation.

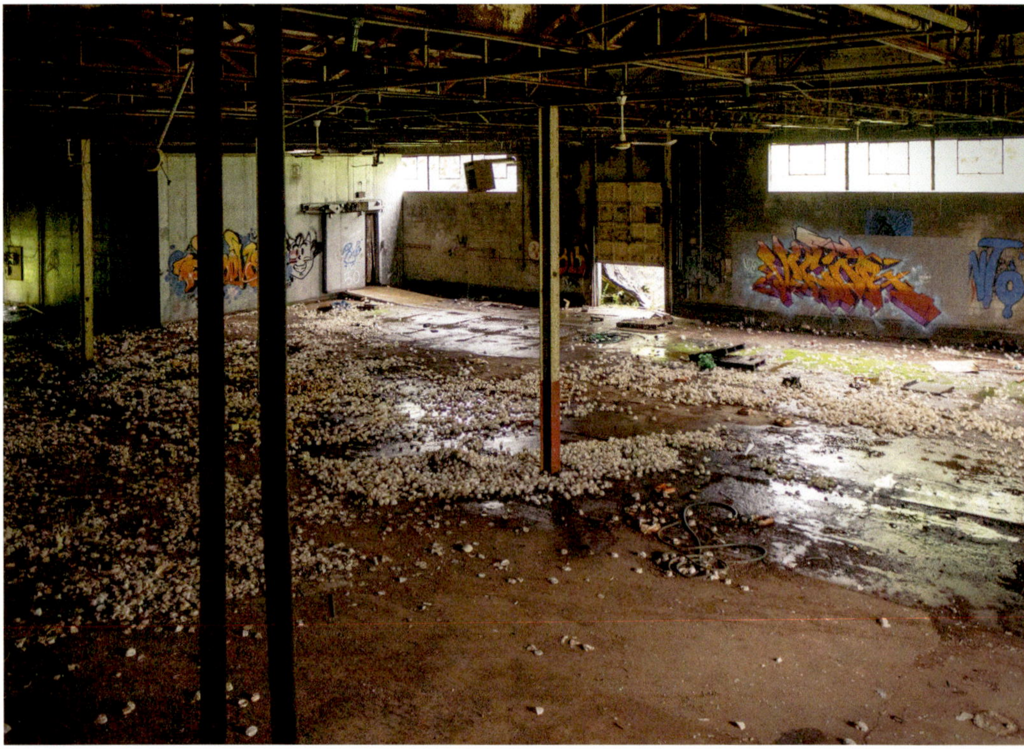

This opening, from the second floor, provides an aerial view of the primary assembly room.

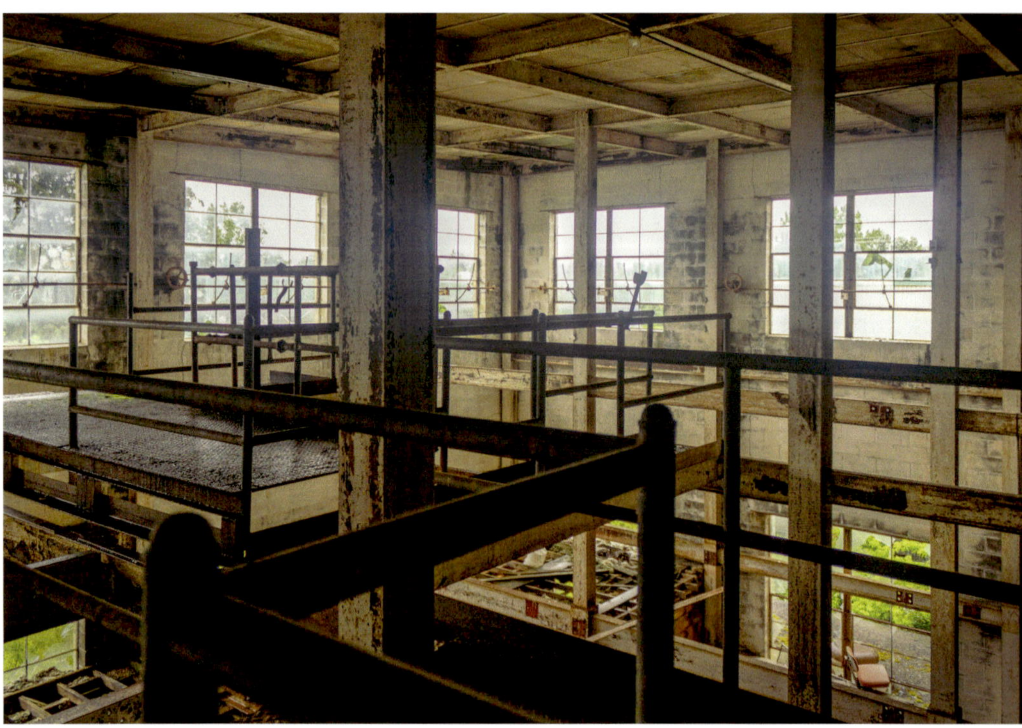

A bird's eye view of the bones of the factory are revealed, as natural light squeezes through shattered windows.

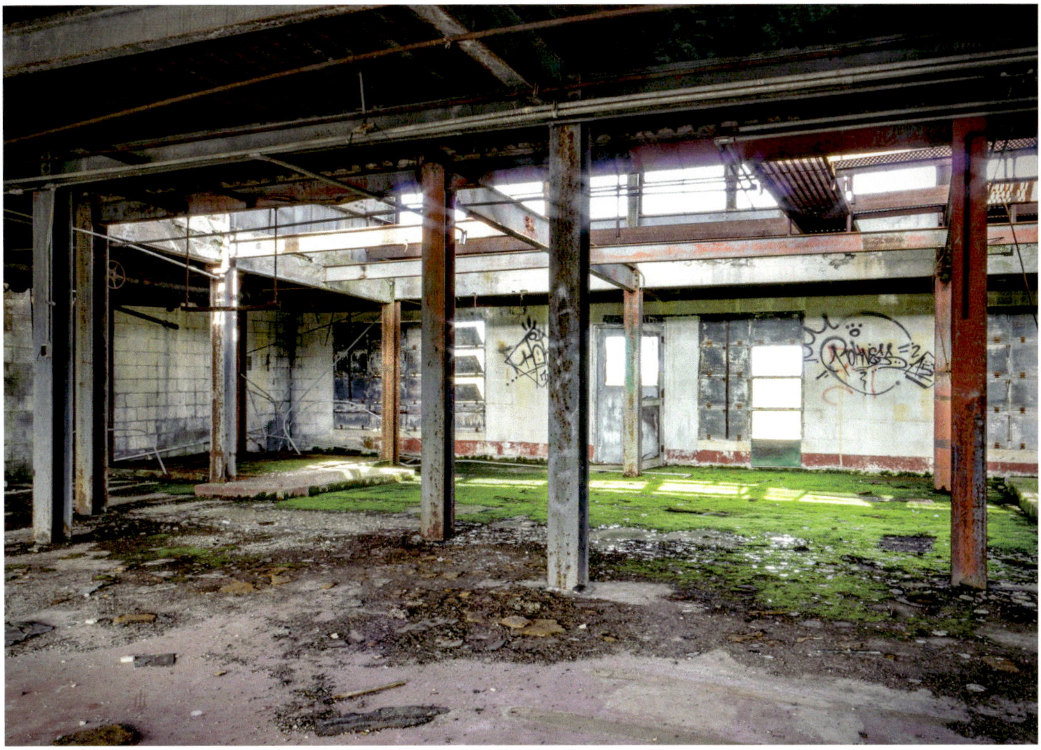

One of many spots, on the third floor, where nature has begun reclaiming her territory.

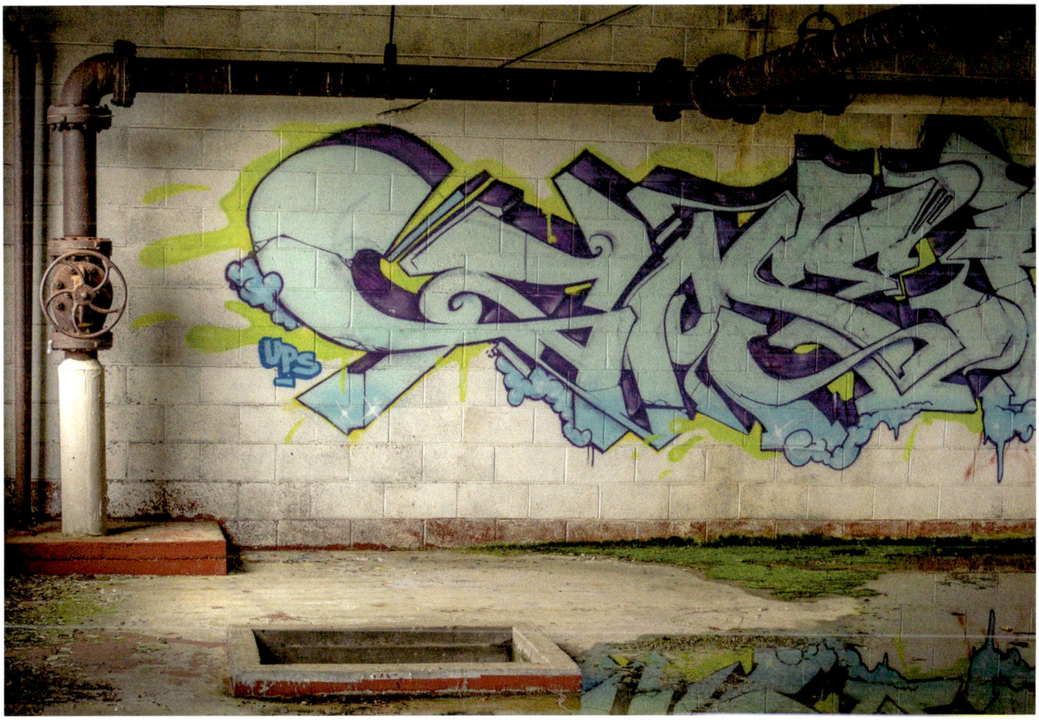

Detailed shot of graffiti, framed by the factory's large pipe system.

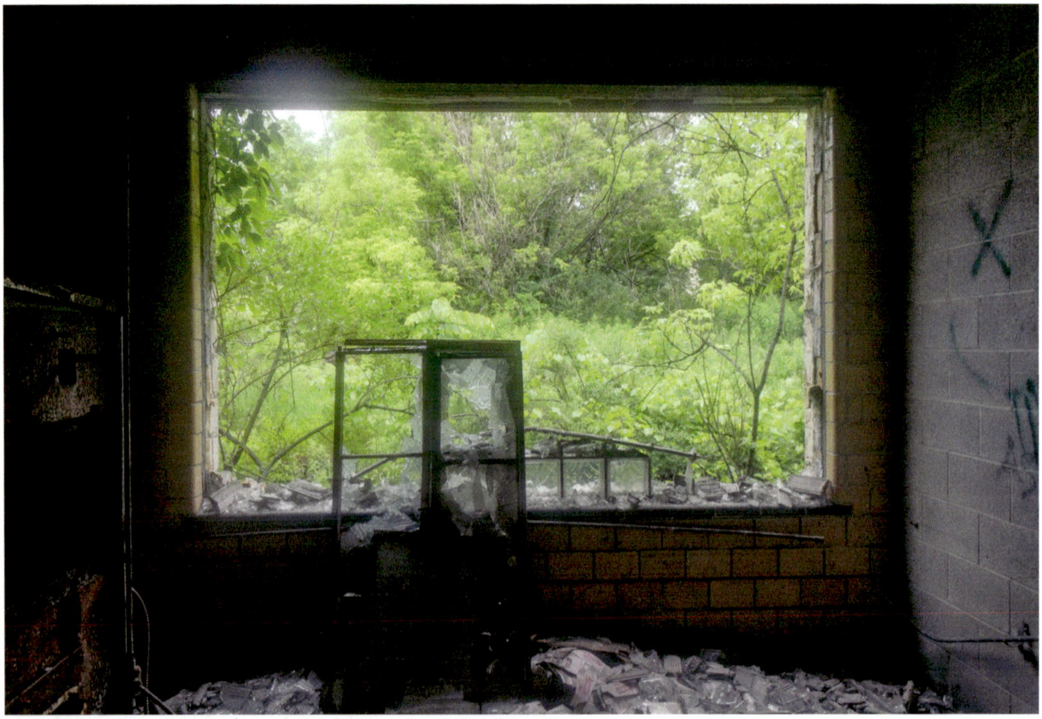

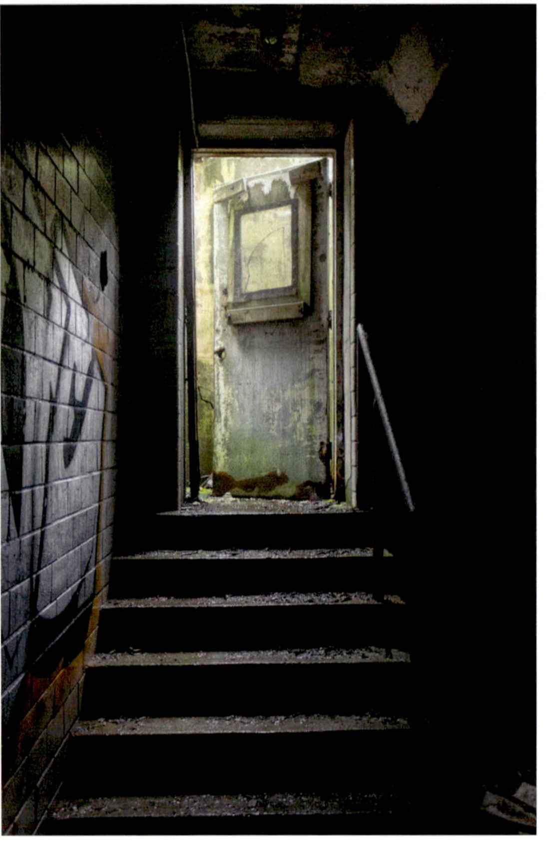

Above: What was once a large glass brick window now serves as an open door for nature to come in.

Left: An open, decrepit doorway acts as the only passage for light to enter the entire basement.

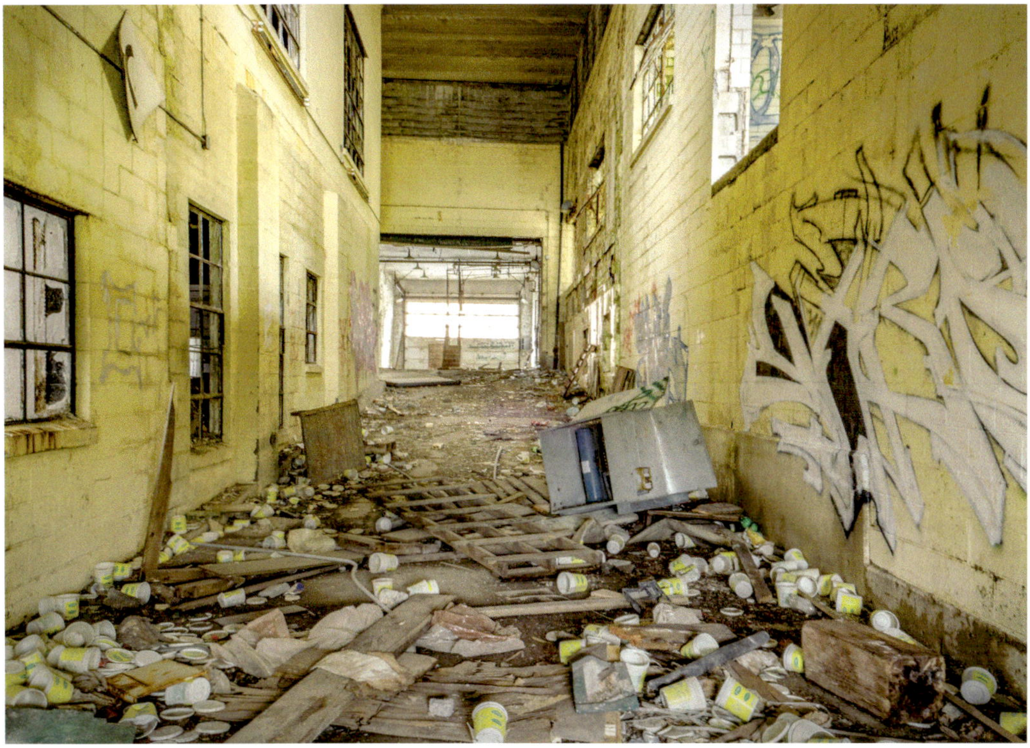

Corridor floor littered with old product containers and debris.

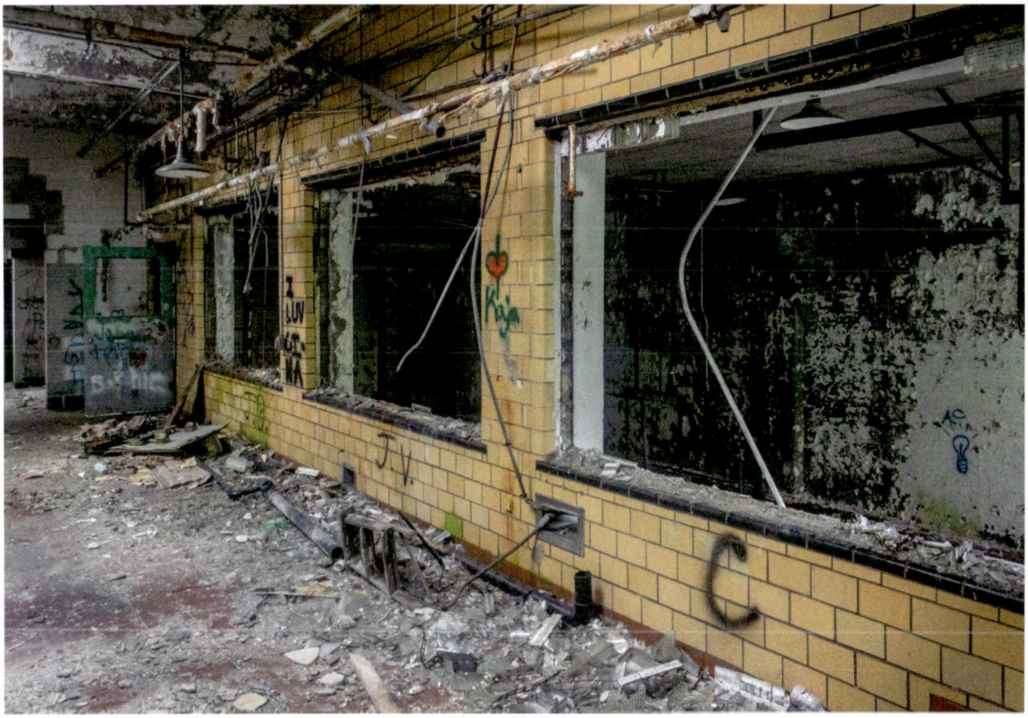

A wall once decorated with bricks of glass, now serves as an alternate view of the loading ramp.

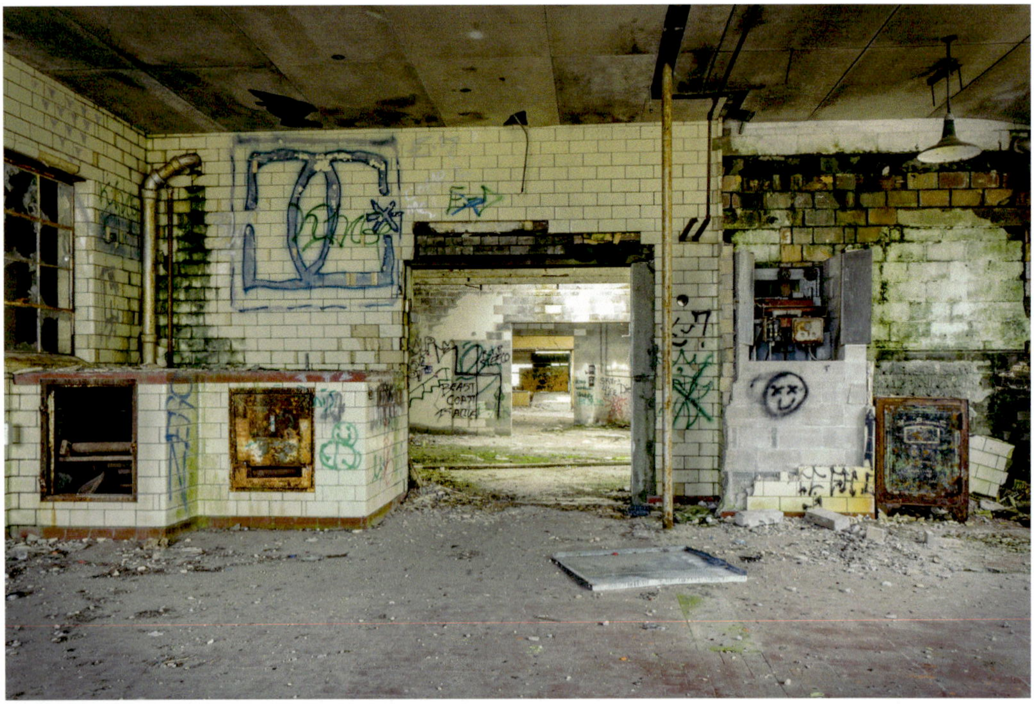

One of the many sections of the second floor, beautifully deteriorated and dressed in graffiti. An old cast-iron safe leaves many explorers tempted by hidden treasures that might lie within.

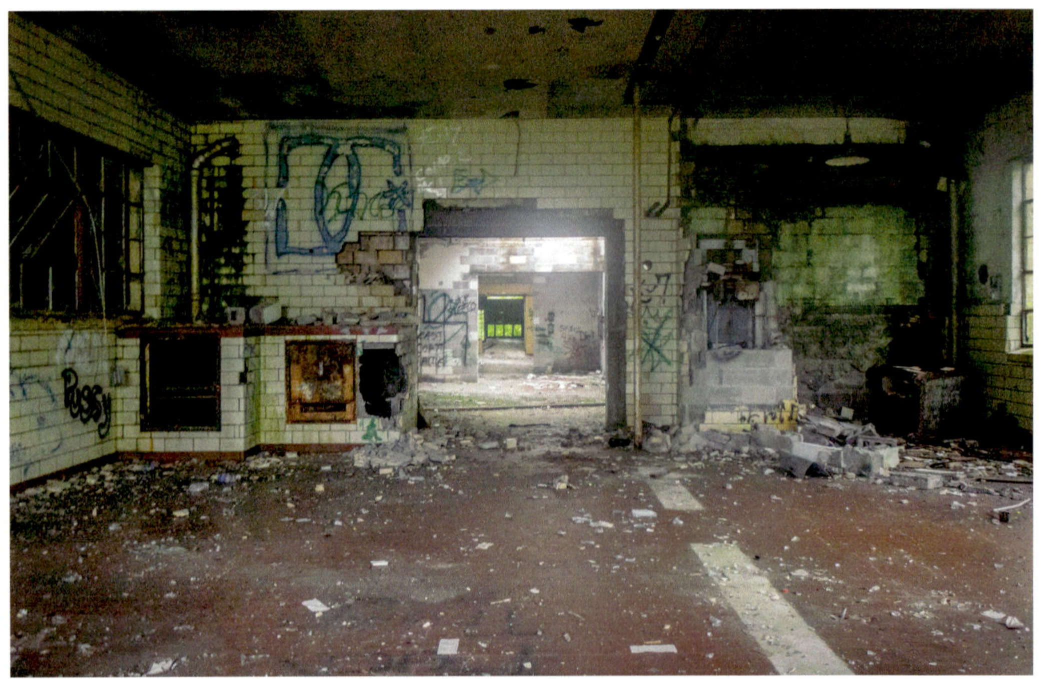

A few months later, I made another visit, to find this once beautiful scene completely destroyed by intruders who succumbed to their temptation. Seeing the aftermath of this left me feeling frustrated and disappointed, for this piece of history was now destroyed.

2

ANTWERP EXPRESSMART

Active Dates Unknown

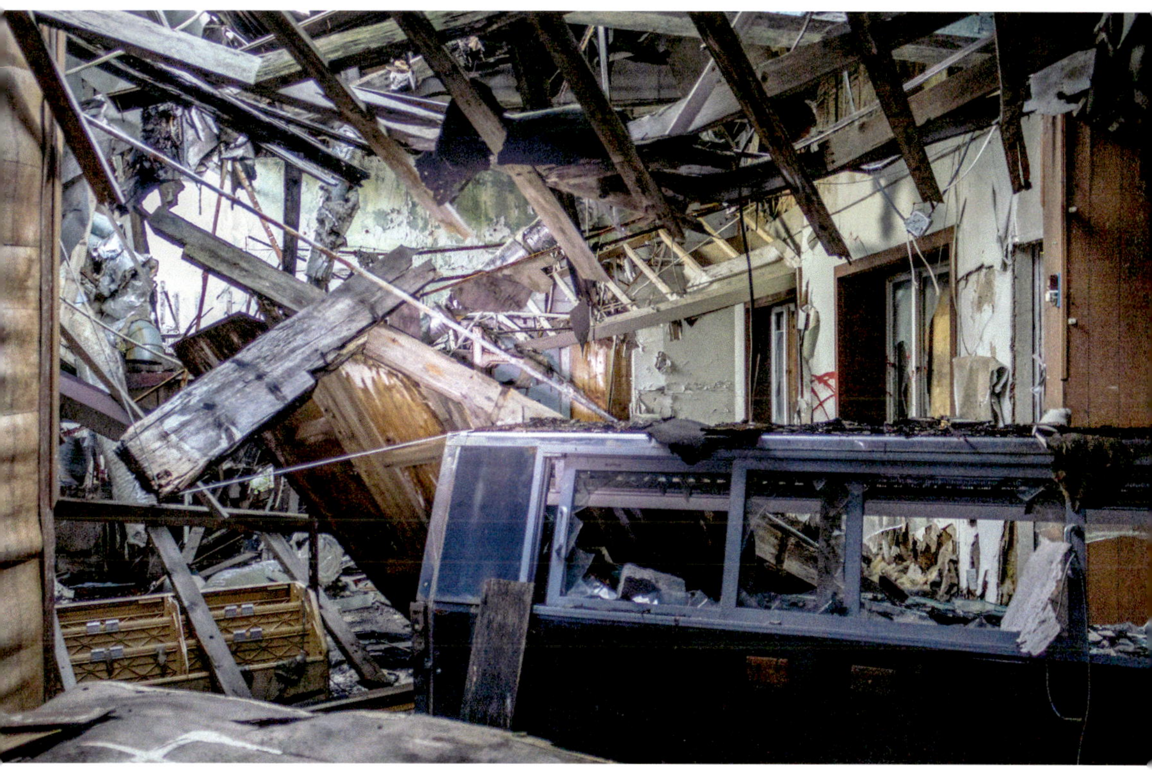

At the edge of a fork in a frequently traveled road lies a sliver of land that once gave life a mini-mart and a small house. The store owner most likely lived in the home. Laboriously, I made my way through the tall grass and into a vacant doorway, to be greeted by a dark, narrow hall, littered with expired mini-mart goods and fallen roof debris. As I gingerly made my way through an obstacle course of fractured wood and wall paneling, I arrived at the heart of the mini-mart. Sadly, the roof was completely caved in. Trudging through roof debris and what remained of the old deli counter, I could see all the old shelves, still bearing some unfamiliar products and goods from before my time. As for the other areas of the mini-mart, they were in the same condition: collapsed sections of roofing with insulation and rusty fragments of metal. I headed over to the neighboring house, which invited me in with its door cracked open. The house, for the most part, lay bare, and rid of any discarded belongings. Evidence of poachers could be seen in every room: cabinets and drawers were ripped wide open, and there was evidence of copper piping having been stripped out for resale. As I made my way upstairs, I was caught completely off guard to find makeshift beds set up with sleeping homeless inhabitants, oblivious to my entry into their refuge.

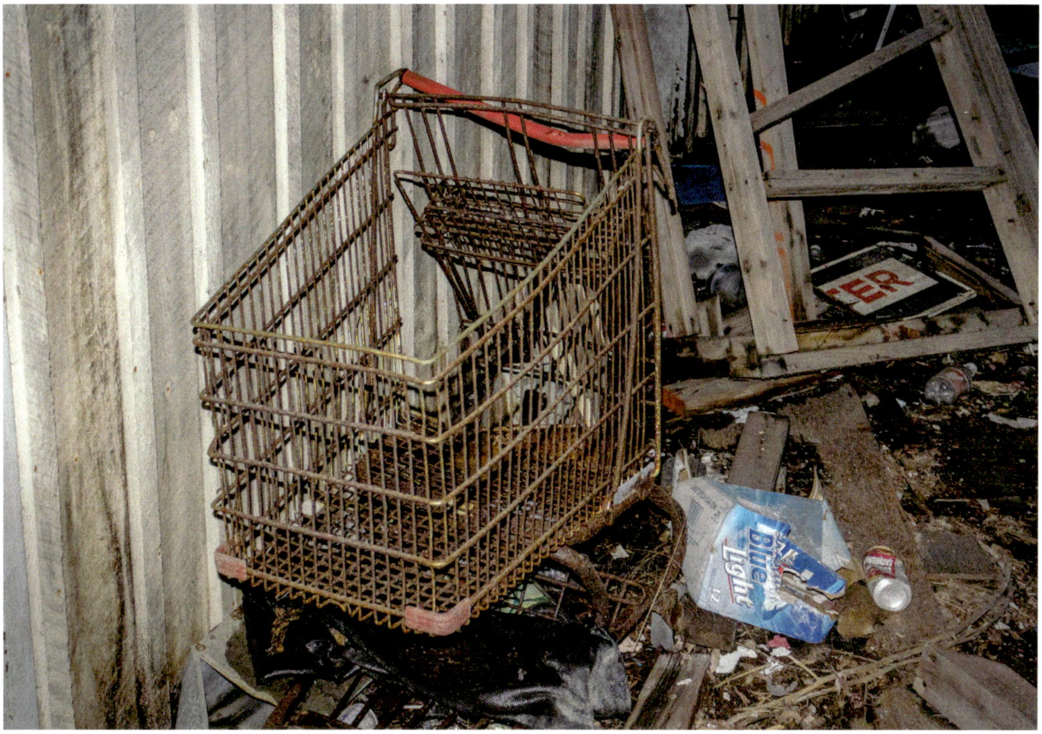

Discarded shopping cart, resting at the entrance of the mini-mart.

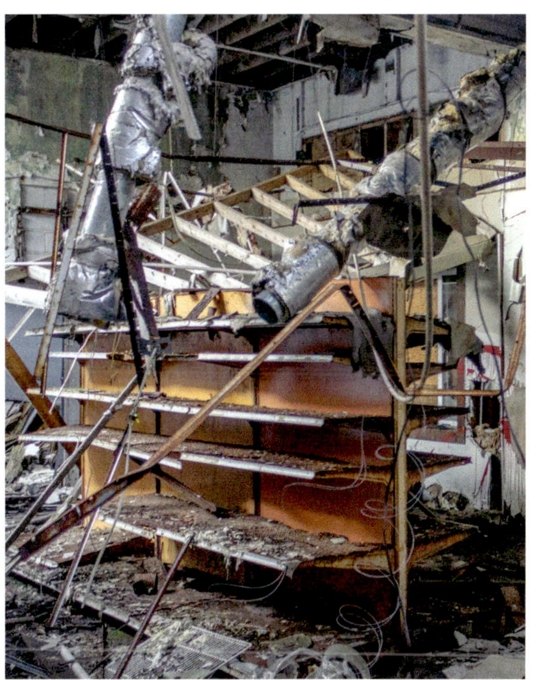

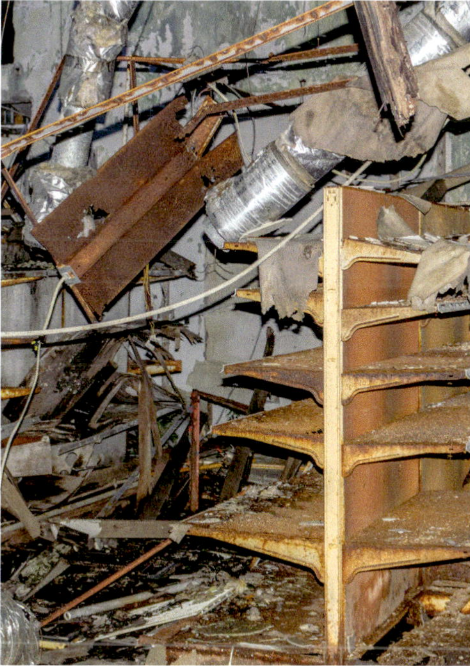

Above left: The other side of the collapsed roof, revealing some empty shelves.

Above right: Dangling metal, rusted screws, and coiled pipes make this area almost inaccessible.

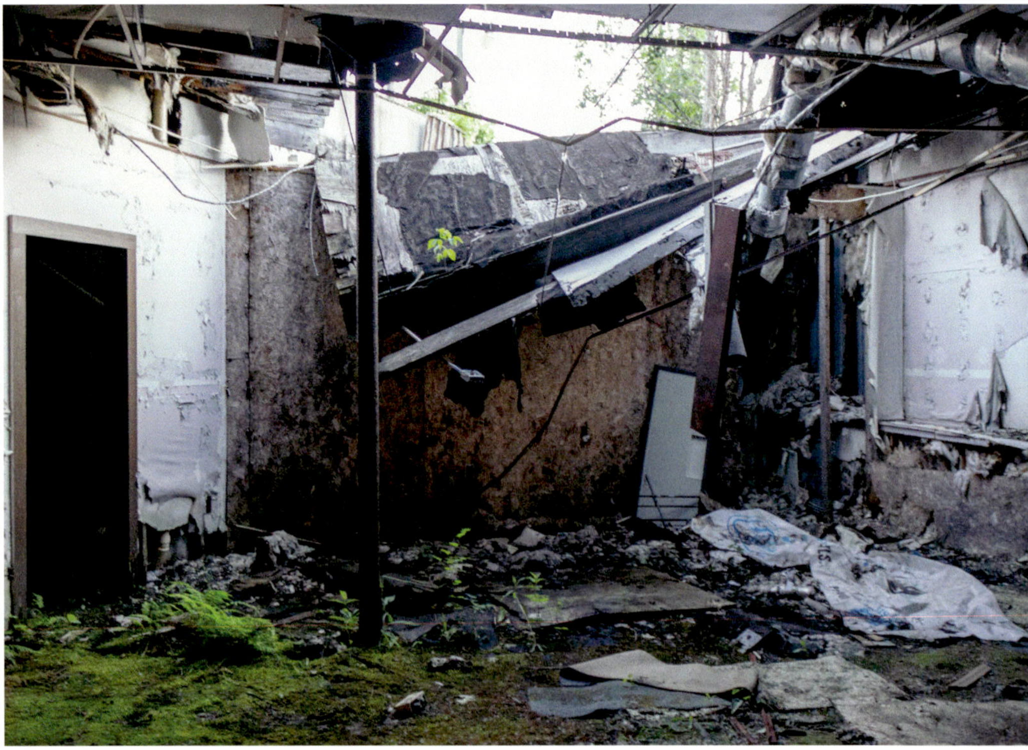

View from the back room of the mart, revealing another section of collapsed roofing.

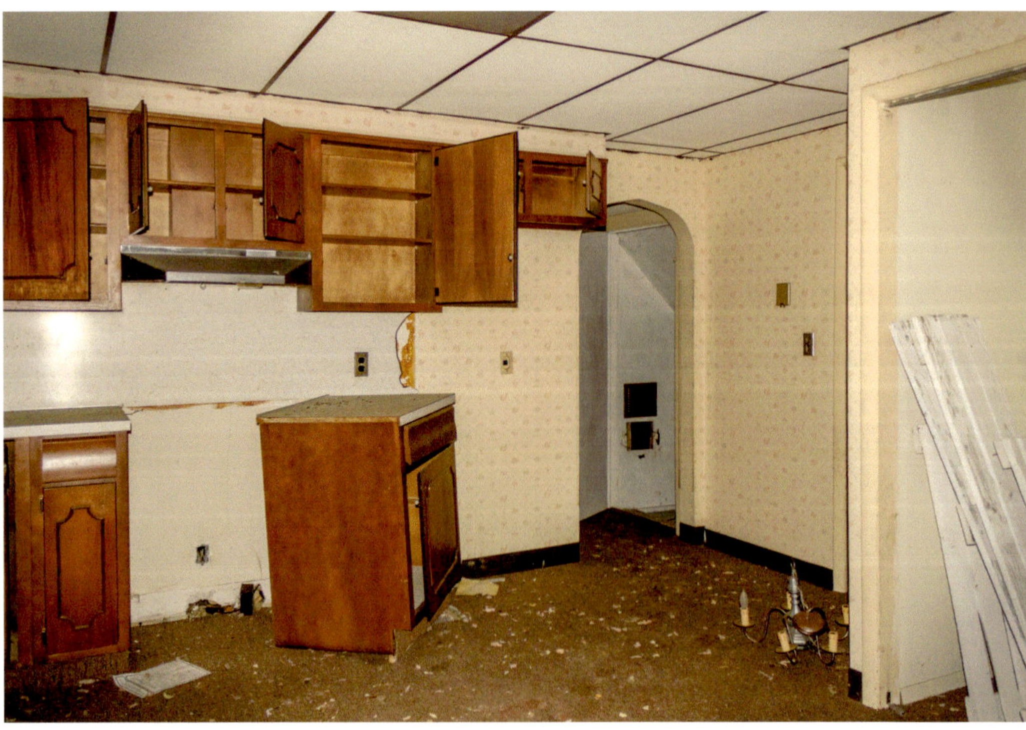

Entrance to the neighboring house; the interior has yet to succumb to severe deterioration.

3

ARSENAL ST. HOUSE

Active Dates Unknown

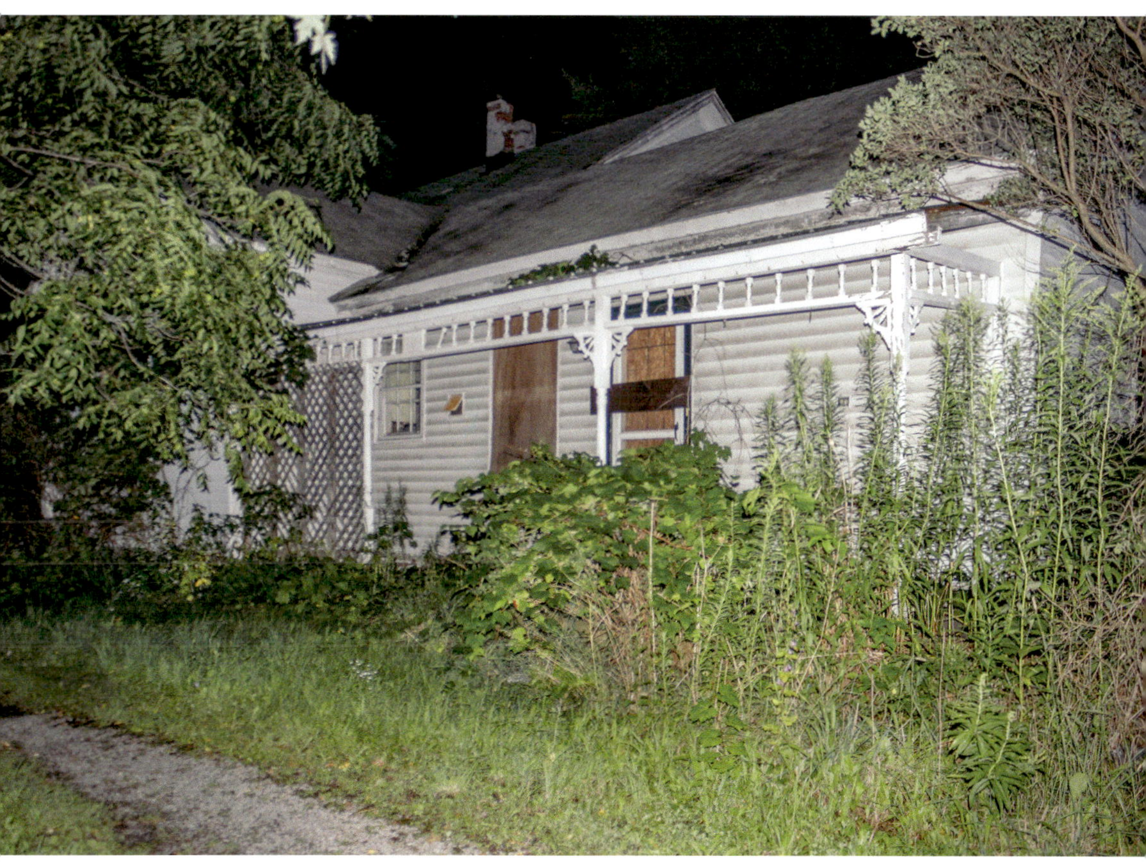

From the home's exterior appearance, nature has already made progress on reclaiming her land. Vines snaked through abscesses in the roof and shattered windows, and vegetation obstructed almost every entry point. I found an accessible cellar door on the porch and made my way down into the stone bowels of the house. With a click of my flashlight I saw nothing but discarded household and lawn equipment. I discovered a preexisting opening, in the ceiling, which once held the staircase leading to the first floor. Luckily, I was able to use an old ladder, leaning against the far-right wall, to gain entrance to the first floor. Stepping into the kitchen, I realized I was not the first explorer to enter this dwelling. Belongings from the previous owners were scattered and smashed all around the rooms, cabinets hung open, and numerous wall holes revealed signs of frustration left by past vandalizers. I traveled deeper and deeper into the house, the structural integrity decreasing as evidence of black mold grew. The closer I got to the attic, the more treacherous my journey became. It wasn't until I climbed the top rung that I found the perpetrator of her degrading condition. A thirty-foot hole in the roof. Rain run-off and moss had been multiplying for what must have been years—trickling down into the second floor, and first floor, before coming to its final resting place in the cellar.

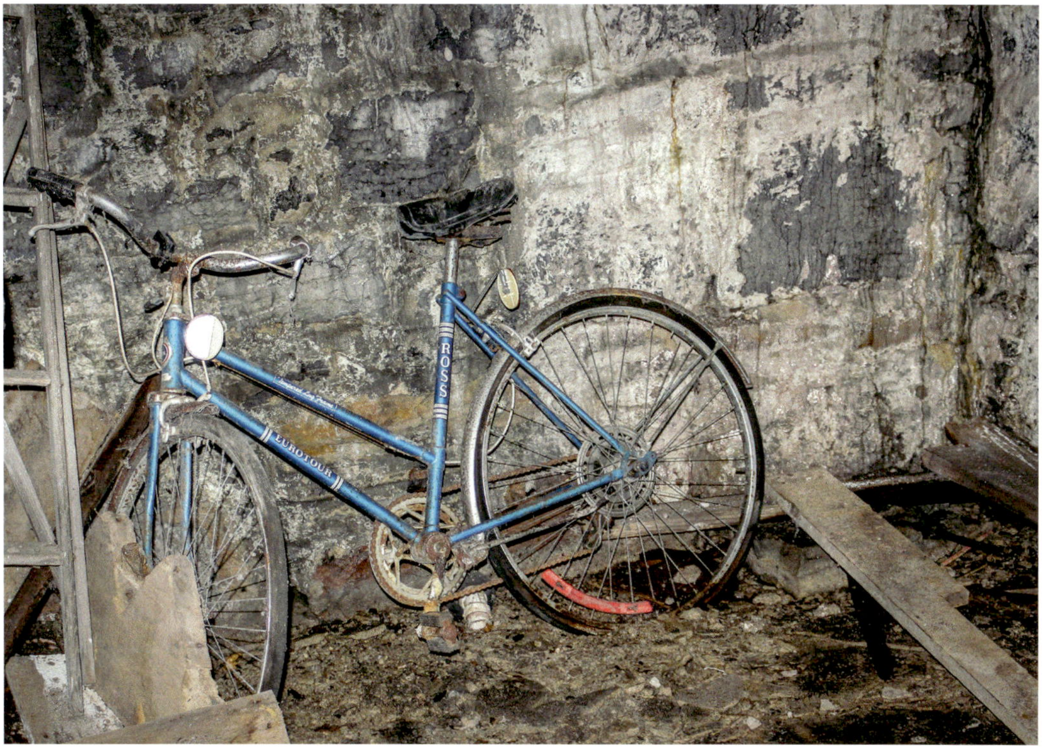

A bicycle retired in the basement of the house.

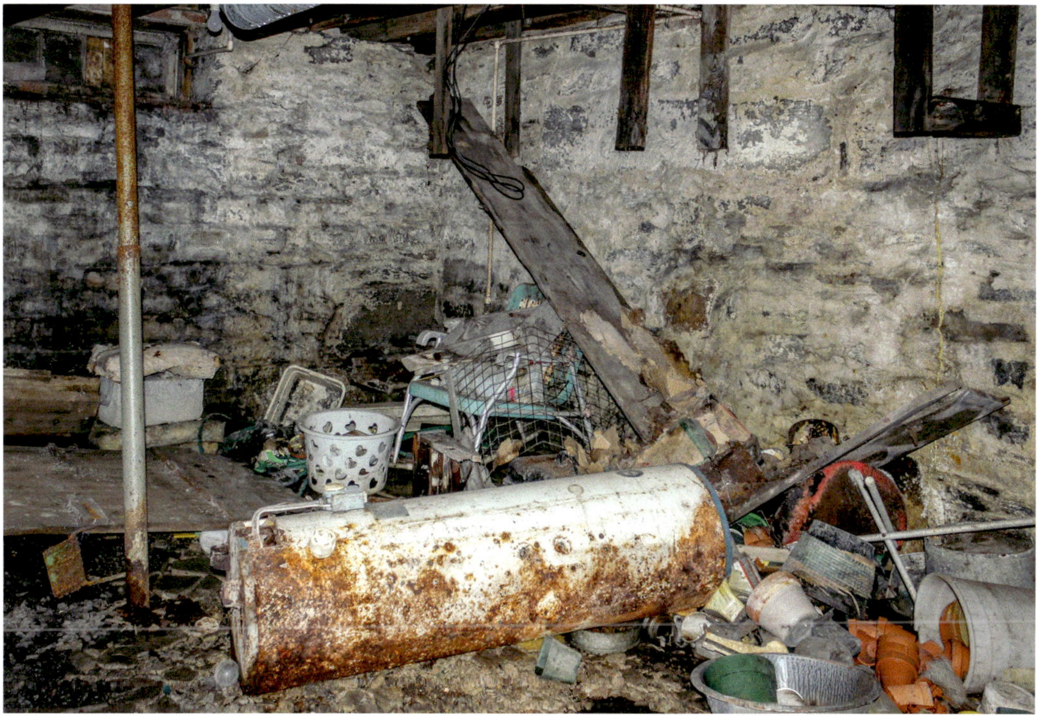

Rusted water heater and lawn equipment forgotten to decay.

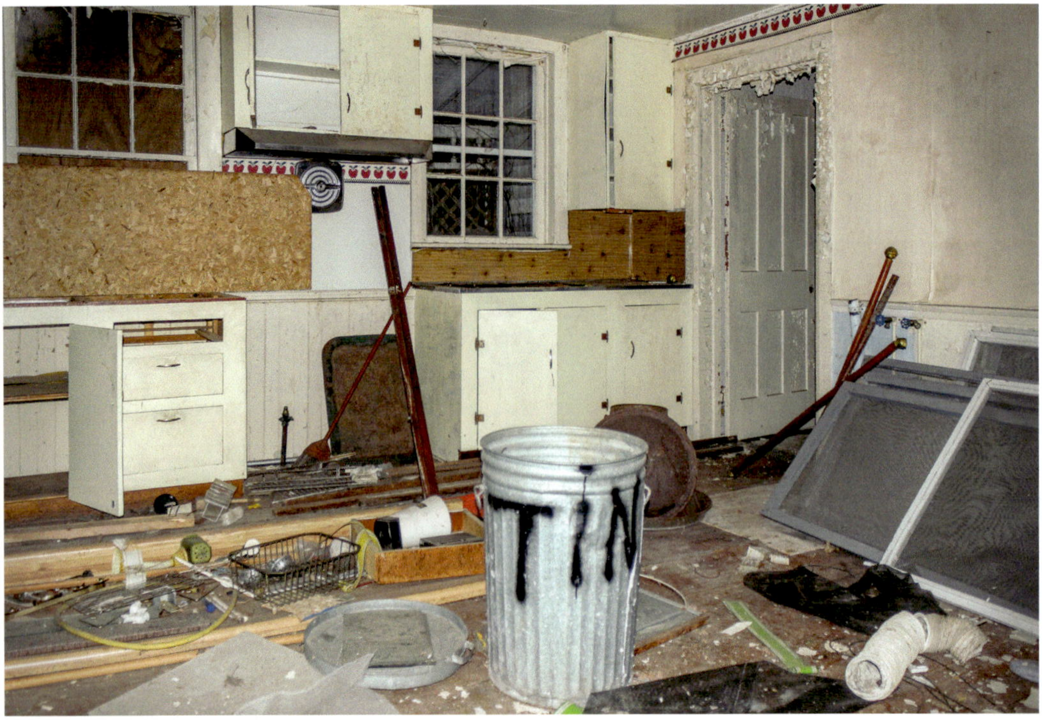

Kitchen of the house, displaying the aftermath of vandals.

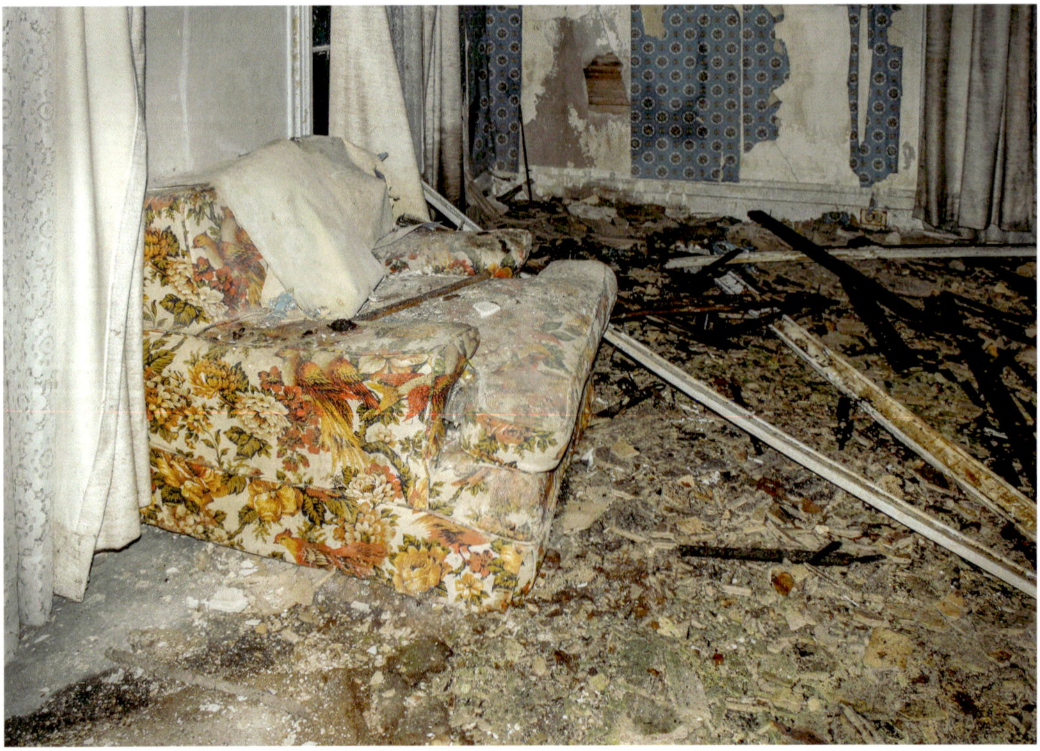

Living room, on the first floor, engulfed in mold from water damage.

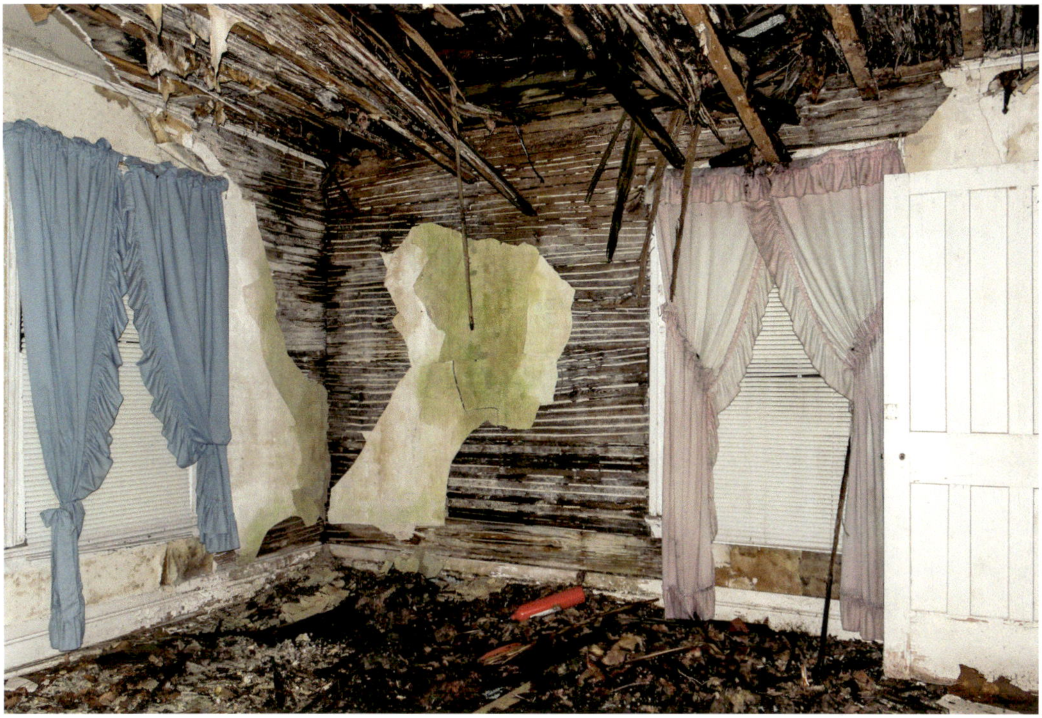

Bedroom, on the second floor, directly below the hole in the attic floor.

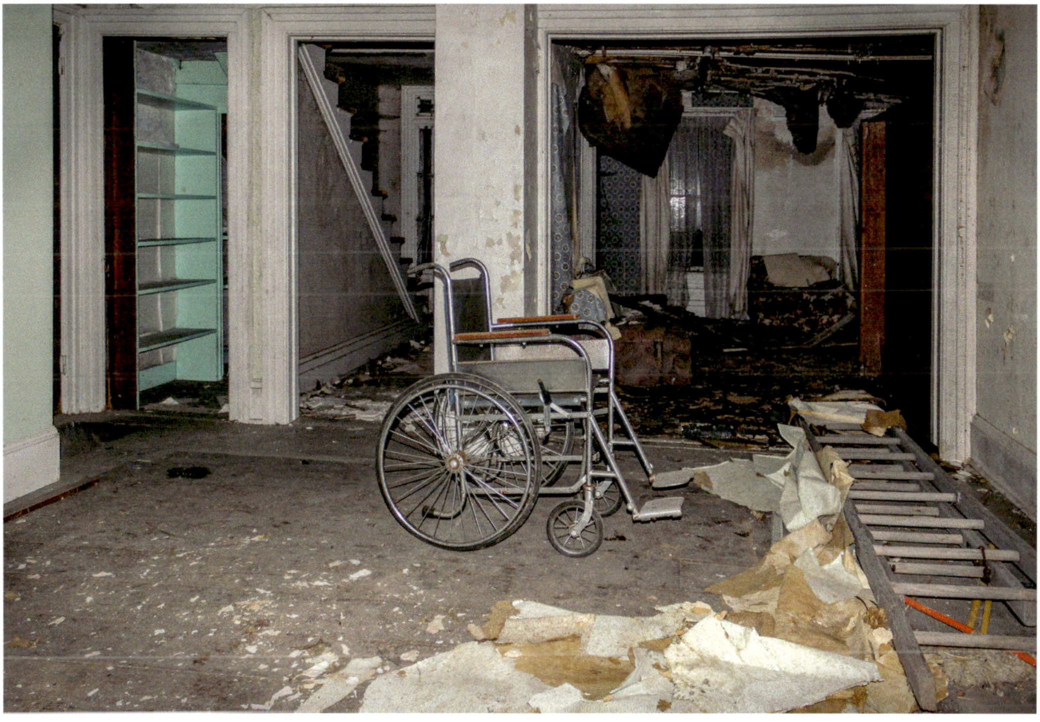

Without bedrooms on the first floor, or handicapped accessible stairs, I was puzzled to see the presence of this wheelchair.

4

COLUMBIA MILLS

1952-1995

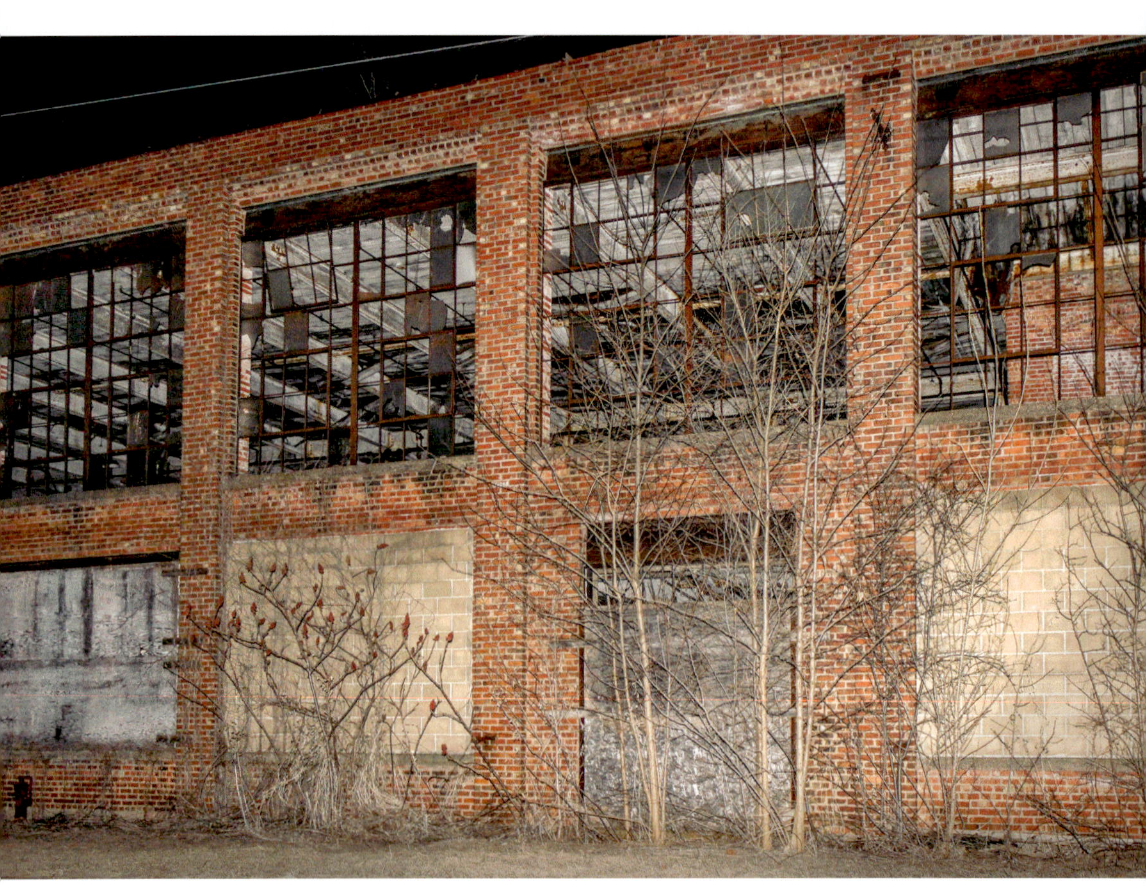

A dominating presence ten feet back from a busy street, this abandoned mill rests and serves as an eyesore for the many locals driving by. For explorers, like myself, this location aroused my senses with its expansive stature and ease of access. It was in January, during winter's chilling grip, that I was made aware of this two-story location, and drove out to find her. Her entry was given away only by the "No Trespassing" sign posted on the land. I pulled over, grabbed my camera, and went in to investigate the interior. Thick snowbanks and old discarded vehicles slowed my entrance to the mill's large horizontal-sliding garage door. The garage door was a few inches thick, with a length of fifteen feet; there was no convincing this door to let me enter. The tracks for the door were held in place by years of rust, topped with a fresh layer of ice. The left side of the door had been pried open to reveal some promise. I sacrificed my bag through the narrow gap then took in a large breath, flattened myself as much as humanly possible, and squeezed through. Thankful for my thick winter coat, my torso and stomach were saved from rusted nails and metal shards. Once secure with my surroundings, I turned on my flashlight and saw nothing but a hollow interior littered with discarded belongings and the remnants from the second floor. To say I was disappointed, not finding a staircase, would be an understatement. However, I found a pile of obsolete computers and bins of folders, where an old document, revealing the name "Columbia Mills" existed. Further research of this mill led to the discovery that the property once consisted of multiple buildings, serving as an extensive concrete milling complex.

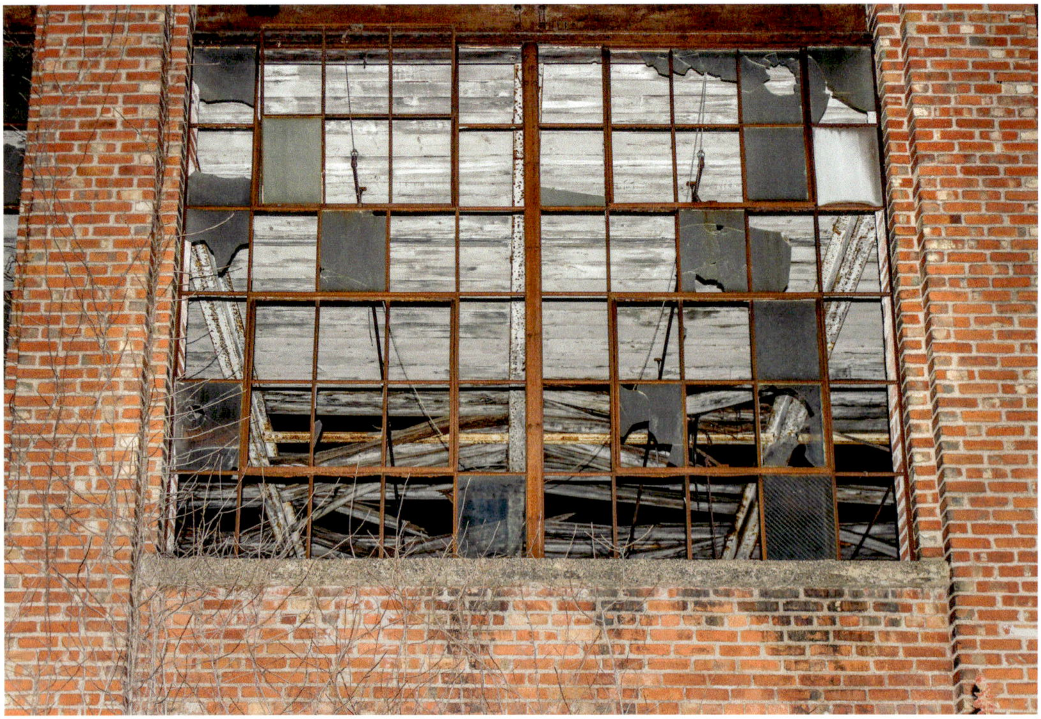

Empty windowpanes reveal the harsh wind conditions of the area, while shattered glass tattles on past vandals.

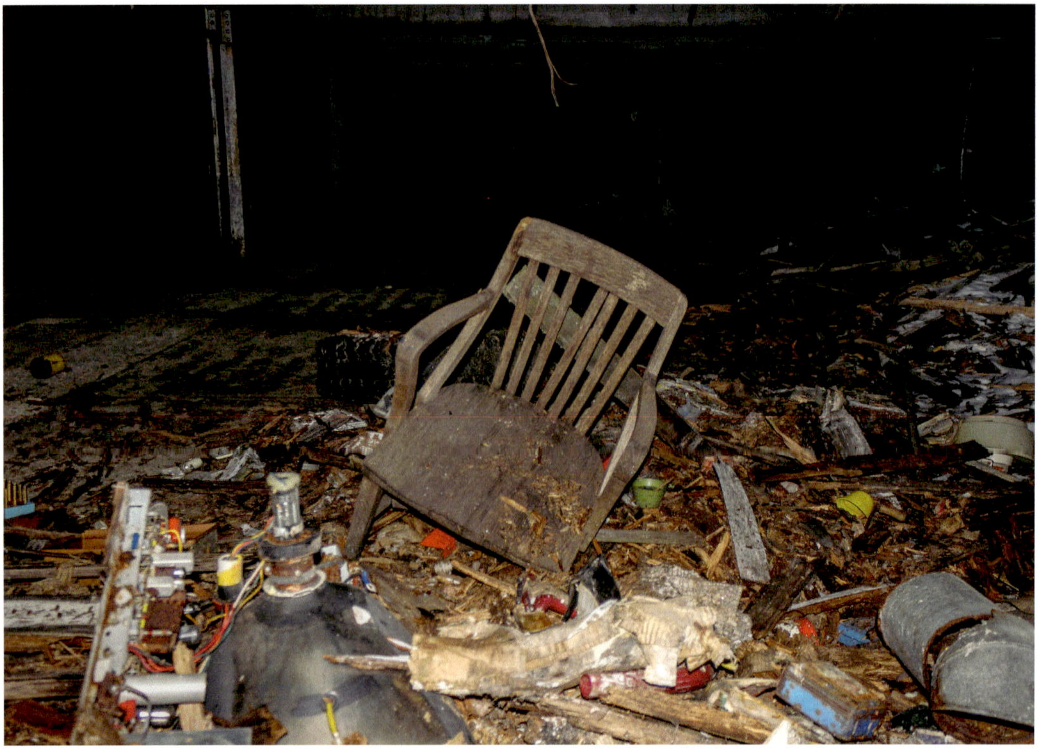

A wooden chair sits in the company of garbage and the remains of an old television.

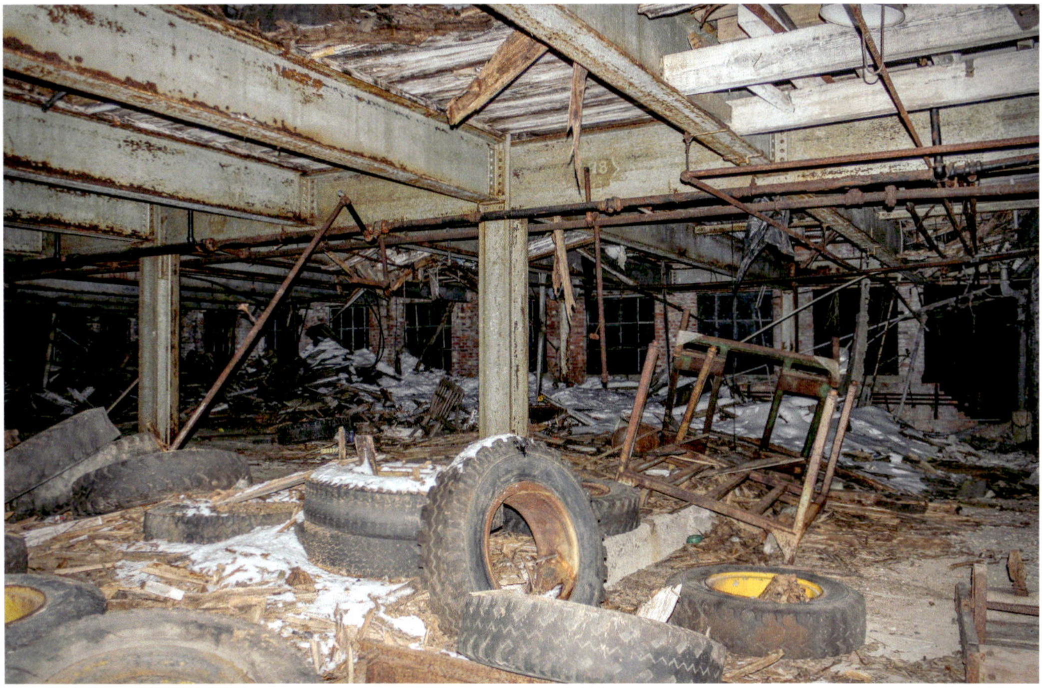

A pile of tires strewn in the middle of the ground floor, appearing to have fallen from above, no longer supported from the floor above.

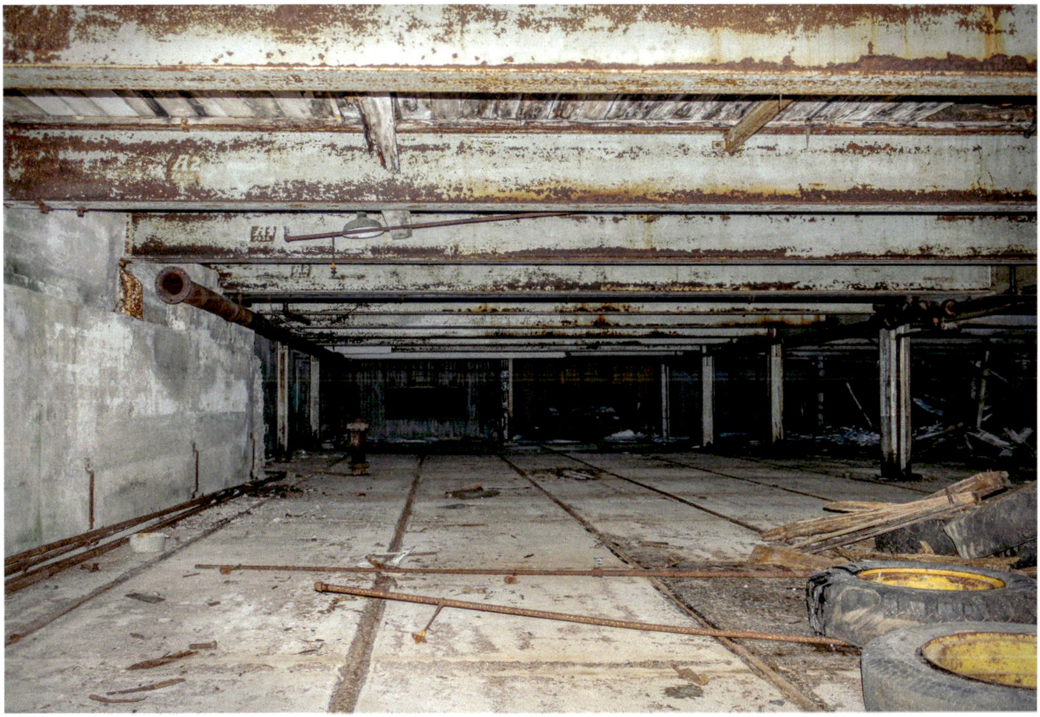

A view down the vast and empty ground level. Numbers on the support beams indicate possible storage sections, evidence of the mill's active past.

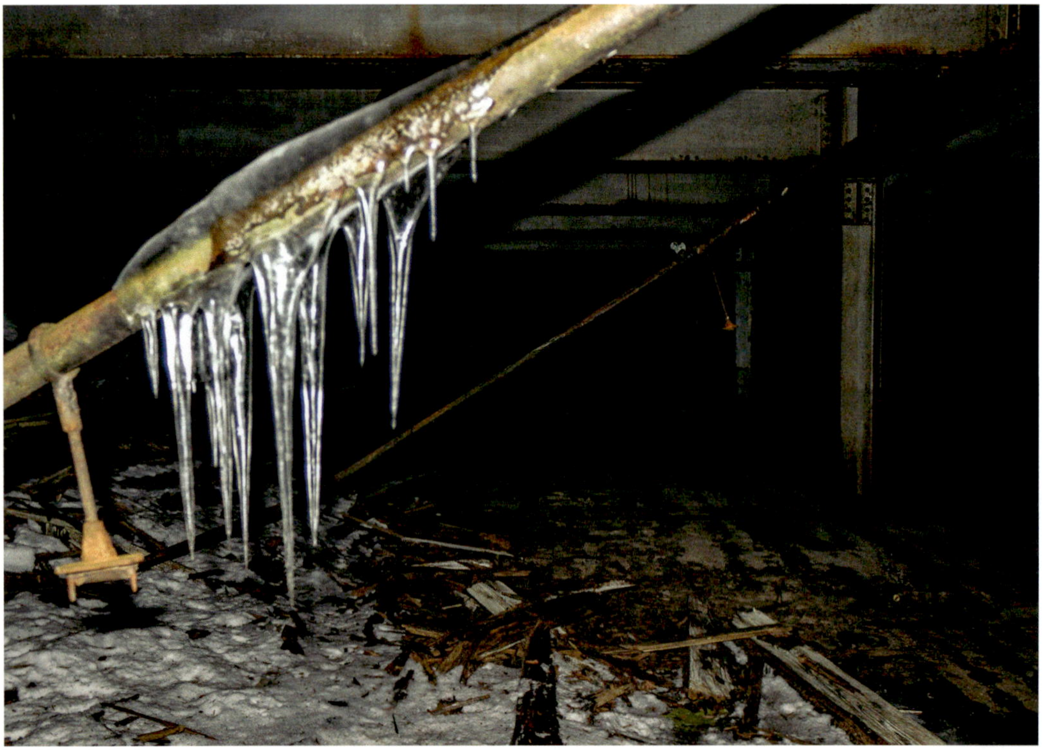

Ice clings onto a fallen pile within an opening of the ground floor.

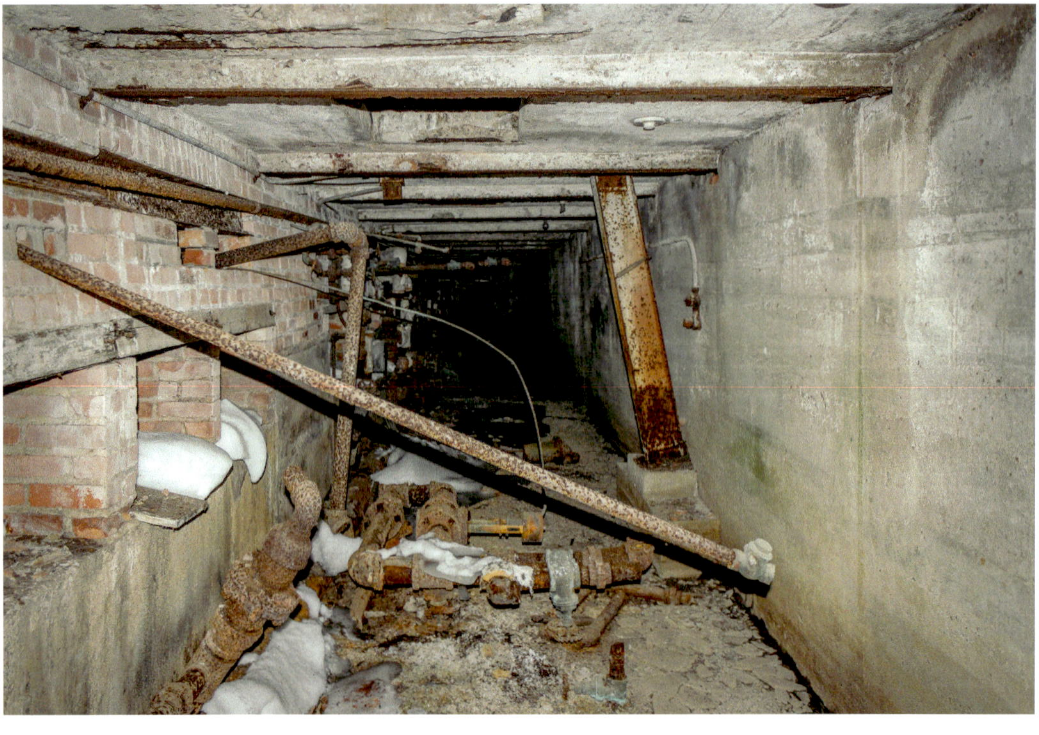

Hidden under the snow, a concrete staircase, leading to a dead-end tunnel, remains a mystery to me.

5

FARMHOUSE

Active Dates Unknown

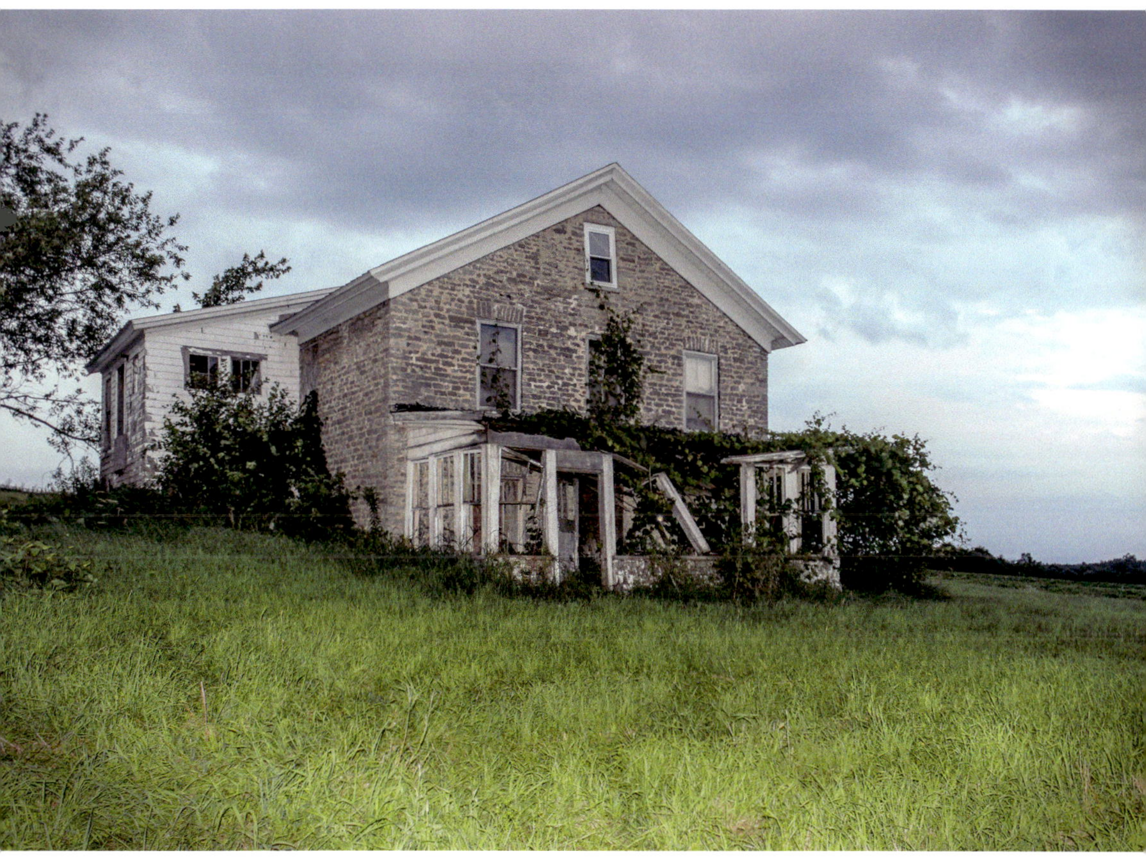

Completely isolated, this forgotten farmhouse sits miles from its neighboring towns, peacefully degrading over the years. While driving down a long back road, I noticed this house immediately. Perched on a hill, receiving shade from only one tree, this house was a sight. The front porch was strangled by foliage while the brick exterior was weighed down with vines and shrubs. Carefully ducking under vines and a rotted porch foundation, I found my way to a door with a large hole, the perfect size for me to crawl through. I entered the kitchen which smelled foul from old produce and was littered with discarded household items. As secluded as she was, this house appeared to have captured the attention of previous vandals and poachers. I made my way to the back of the kitchen, to find an abundance of old glass Pepsi bottles, surprisingly in good condition. After a quick scan of the dining room, I went upstairs to the second floor. Waiting to greet me, at the top of the staircase, was an old plastic teddy bear. An old television set, unscathed by vandals and unlike any I had seen before, was in astounding condition in comparison to the rest of the living room. The remainder of this farmhouse was ransacked and destroyed, a sad reality of time and past intruders. Discovering the old television and Pepsi bottles, I was able to gain bits of cool insight to life before my time. This is what fuels my enthusiasm and drives me onto more explorations.

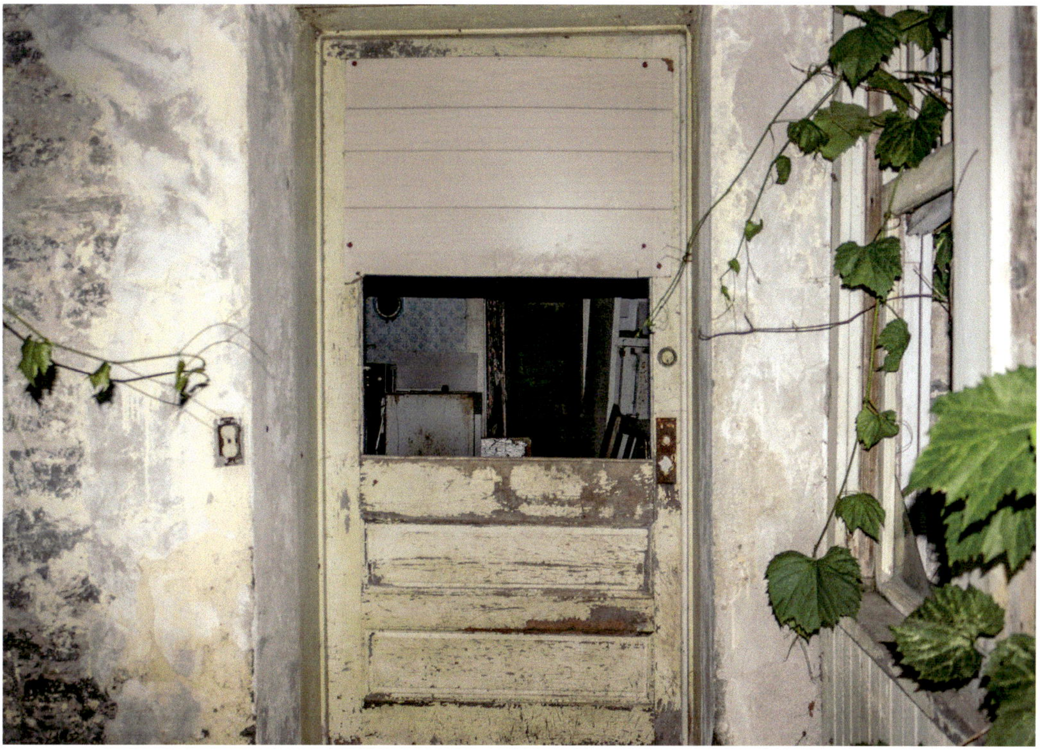

Front entrance to the farmhouse; an opening in the door provides explorers with an entrance through the sealed door.

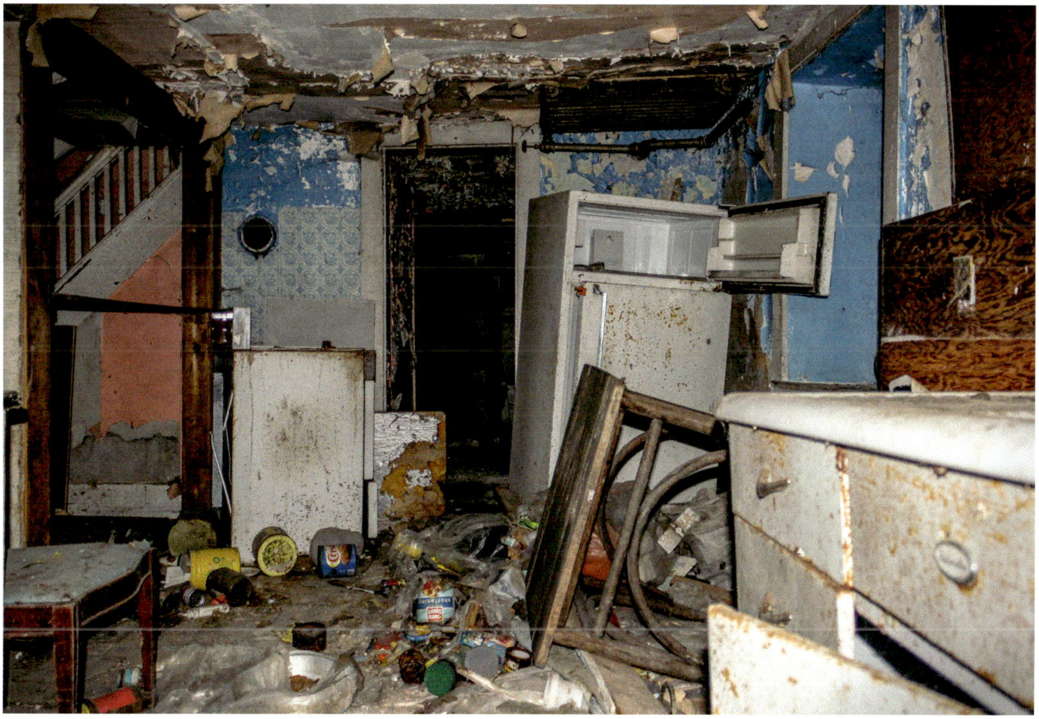

A glimpse of the kitchen and back hallway, littered with expired goods and waste.

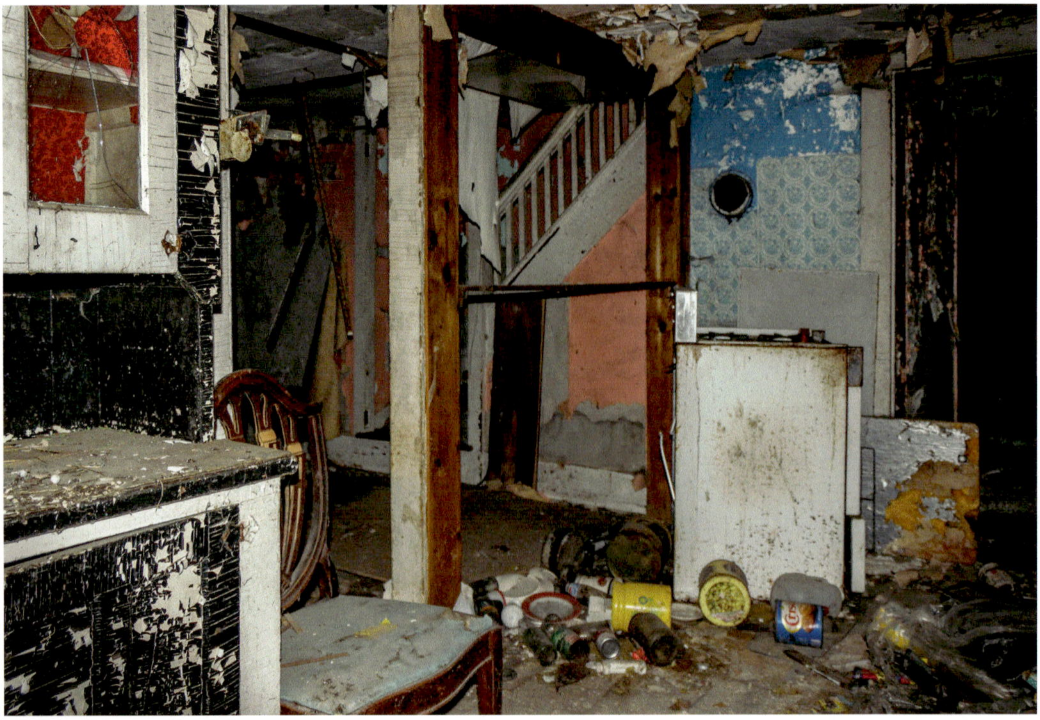

The degrading state of the interior reveals numerous stories with its layers of wallpaper that had been applied throughout this house's lifetime.

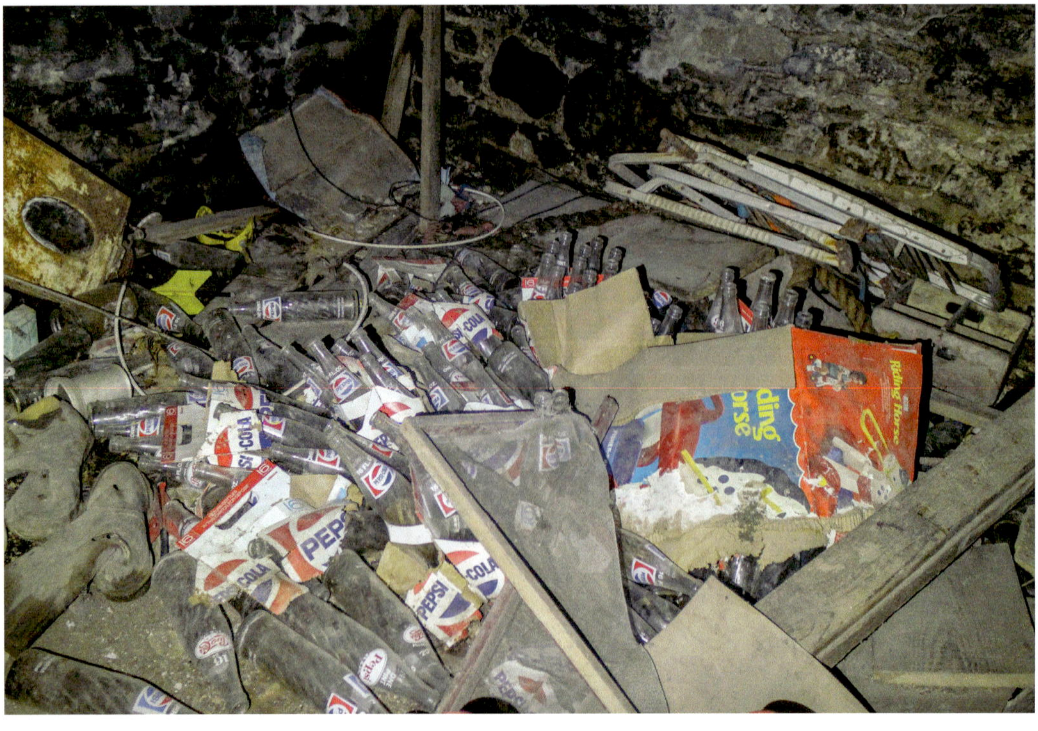

A pile of old Pepsi bottles, surprisingly intact, given all the debris and vandalism.

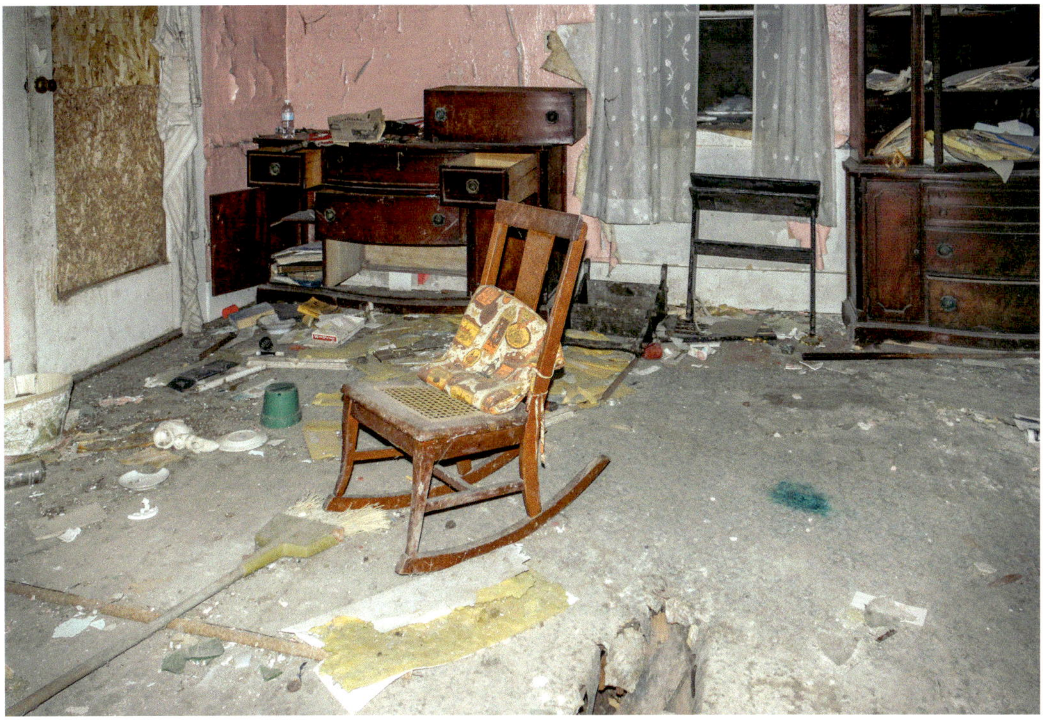

A lone rocking chair sits in the middle of the deteriorated dining room.

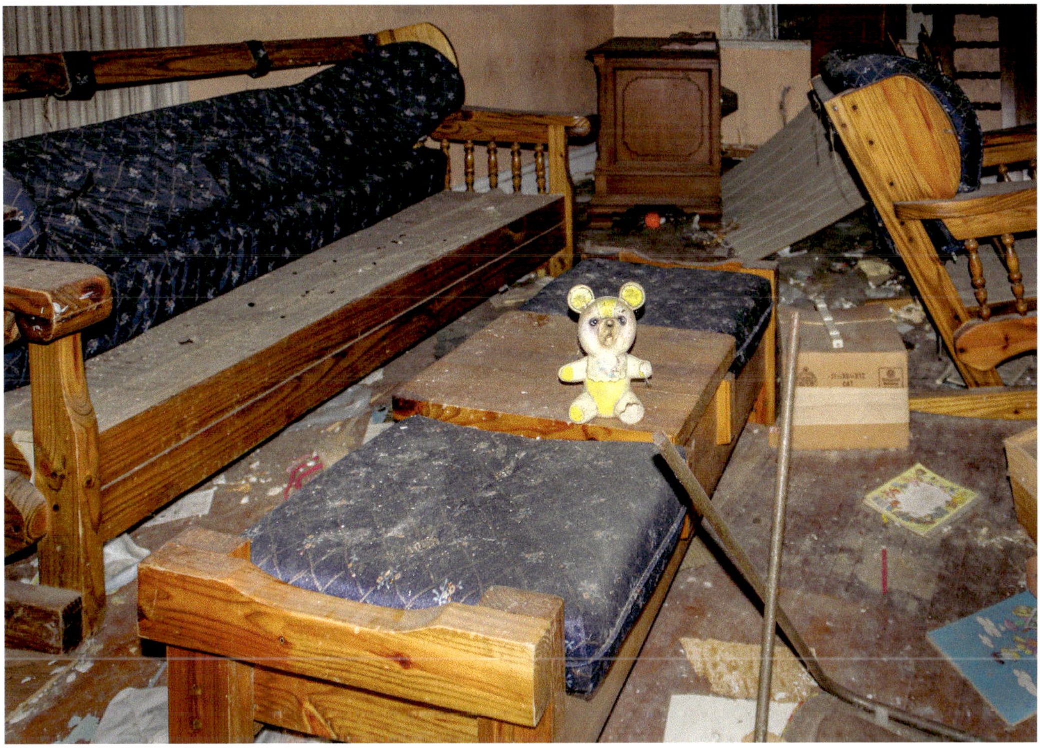

A small bear happily greets intruders as they enter the second-floor living room.

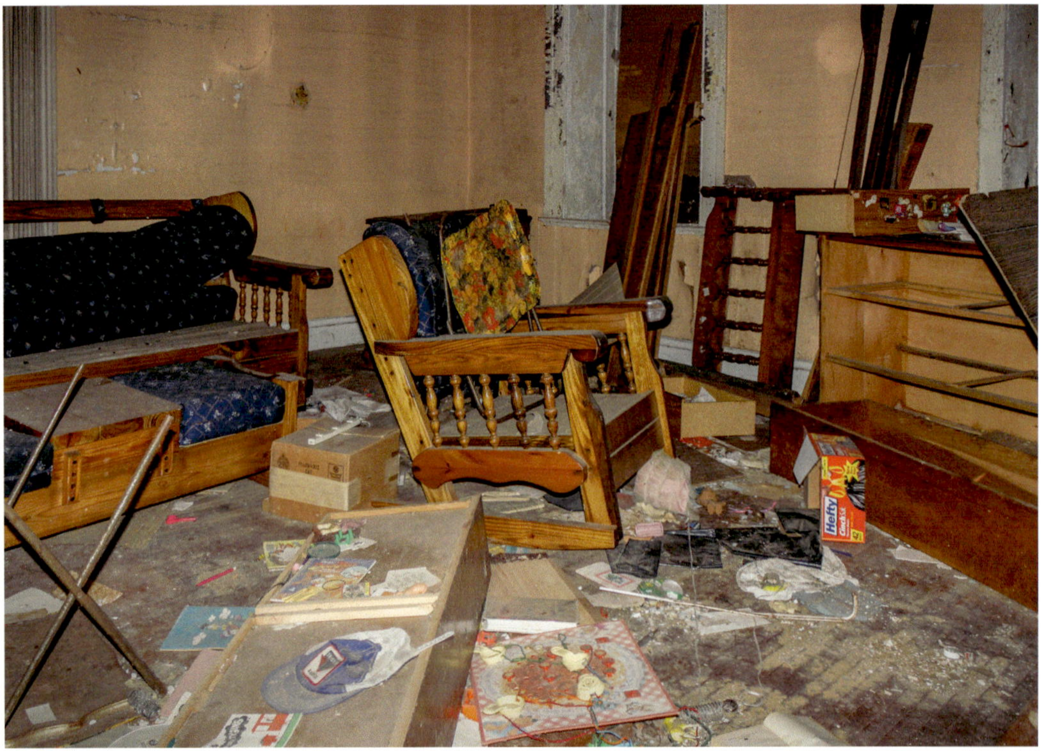

The beautiful woodwork and furniture appears to have been protected from vandalism.

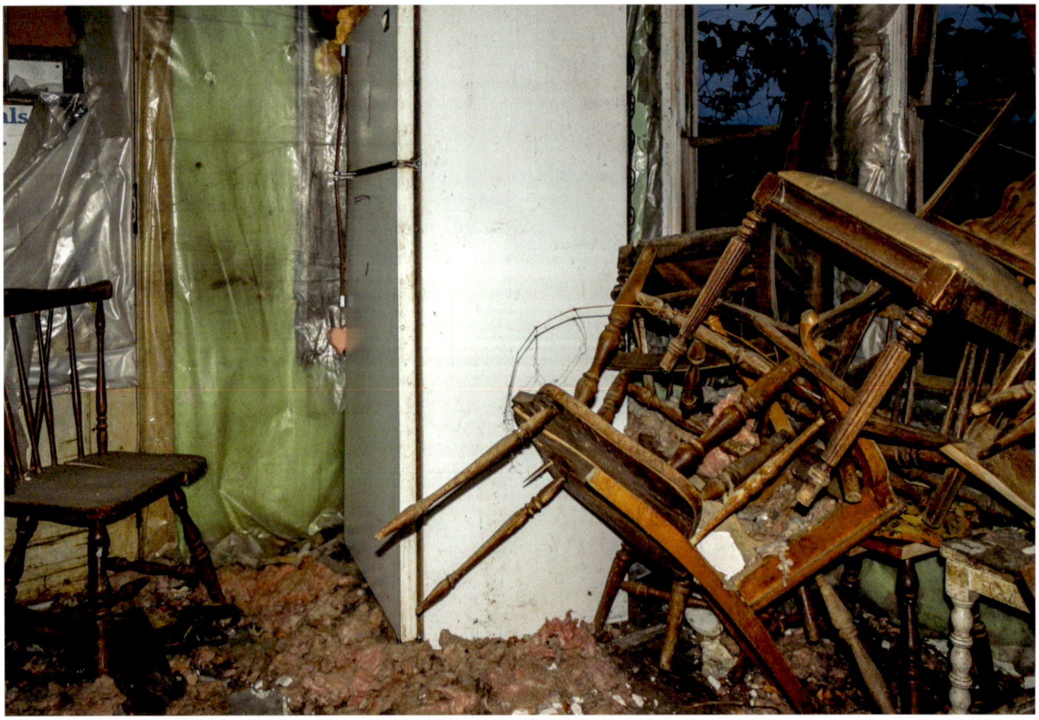

Chairs crammed up against a fridge, engulfed in insulation and mold.

6

PRICE CHOPPER

Active Dates Unknown

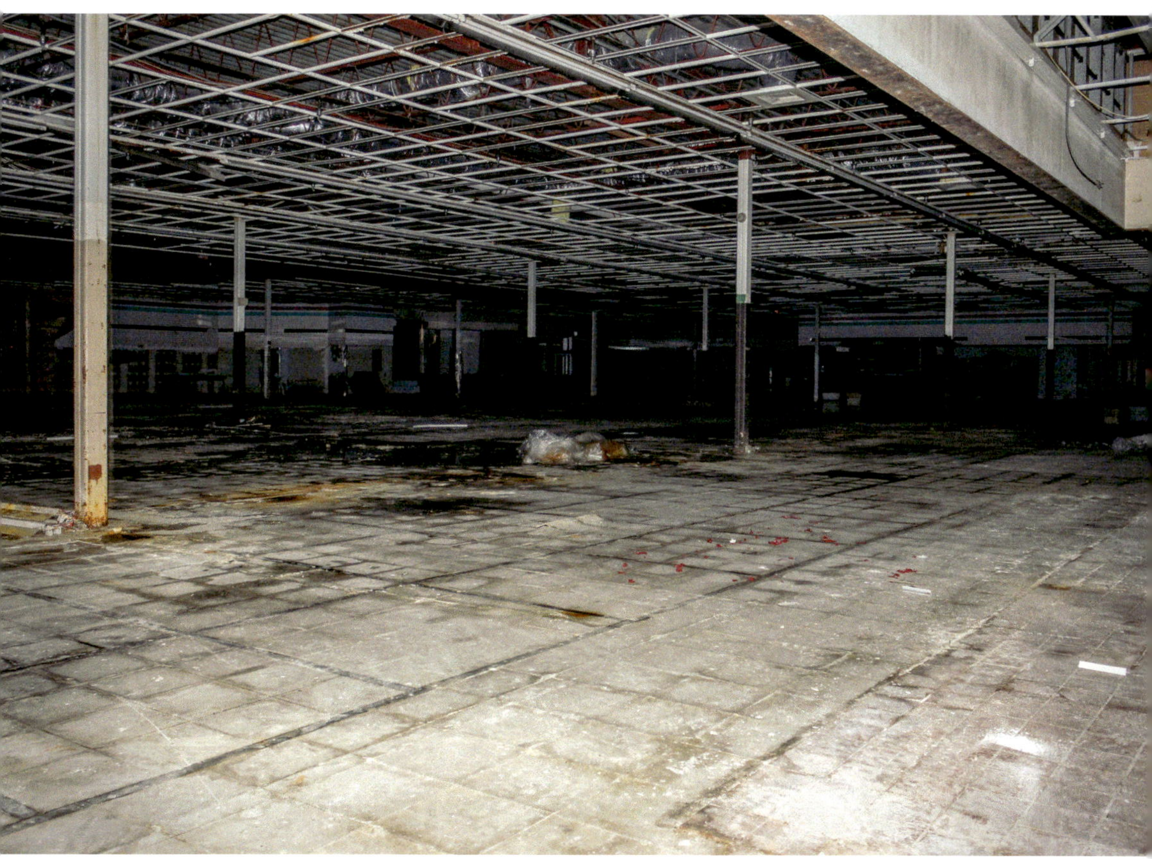

The grand stature of this grocery store's exterior overwhelmed my desires to get a glimpse of the inside. Determined to find an entrance, I walked around the parameter of the building, four to five times, in search of an entrance. Ready to call it quits and head home, I spotted a silhouette of an open latch on the roof. Normally, I wouldn't attempt to scale the side of the building and find my way on to the rooftop, but the size of this building was too much for me to give up on. I made my way over and down into the empty Price Chopper. The sound of my feet hitting a rusted ladder echoed throughout the building. Once inside I experienced something I had never experienced before—complete silence. There was no wind, crickets, animals, or street noise. Every step I took and breath I made was amplified throughout the entire building. Once I was accustomed to the quiet, I found it rather peaceful and soothing. I ventured into the opening of the grocery store, feeling abnormally relaxed. When I pointed my flashlight across the opening, I realized that my light didn't reach the far end of the building. Unsure of what could be waiting for me on the other side, I covered the perimeter of the building before working my way into its center. Sadly, there was nothing more to this building aside the empty shell of what it used to be. Here this shell laid, littered with little pieces of equipment, and tools and trash scattered here and there in selective spots around the building. There was not much historical significance to be found within this Price Chopper, but I still appreciate exploring this former grocery giant.

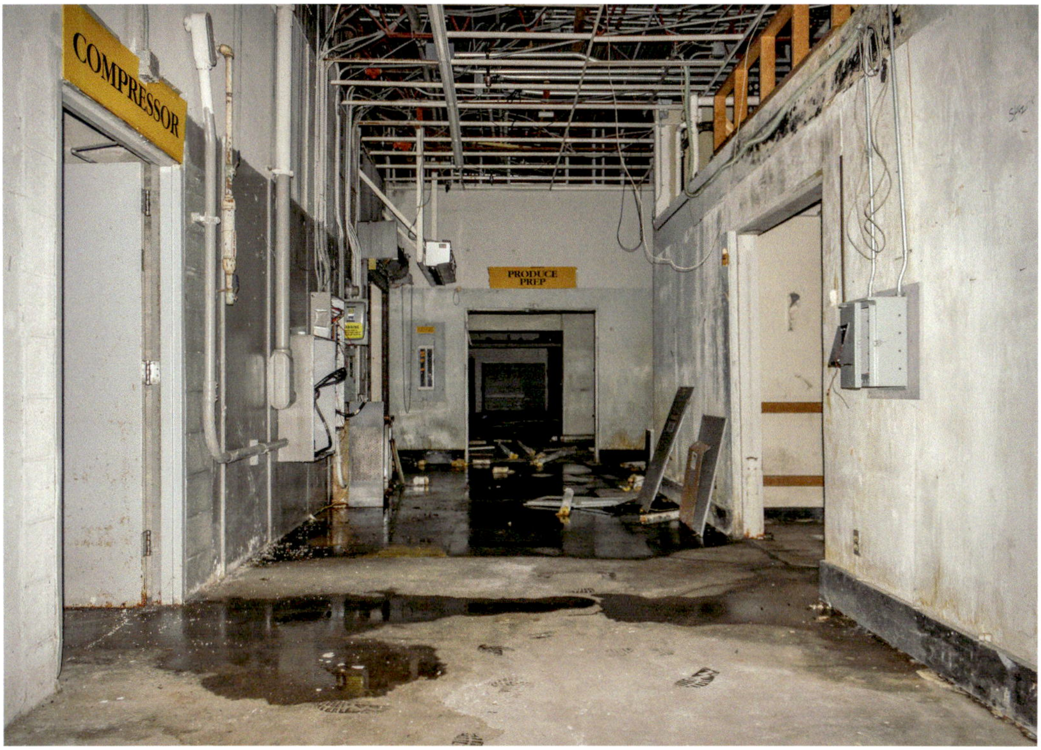

A glimpse down the back hallway at rooms customers would most likely never have seen.

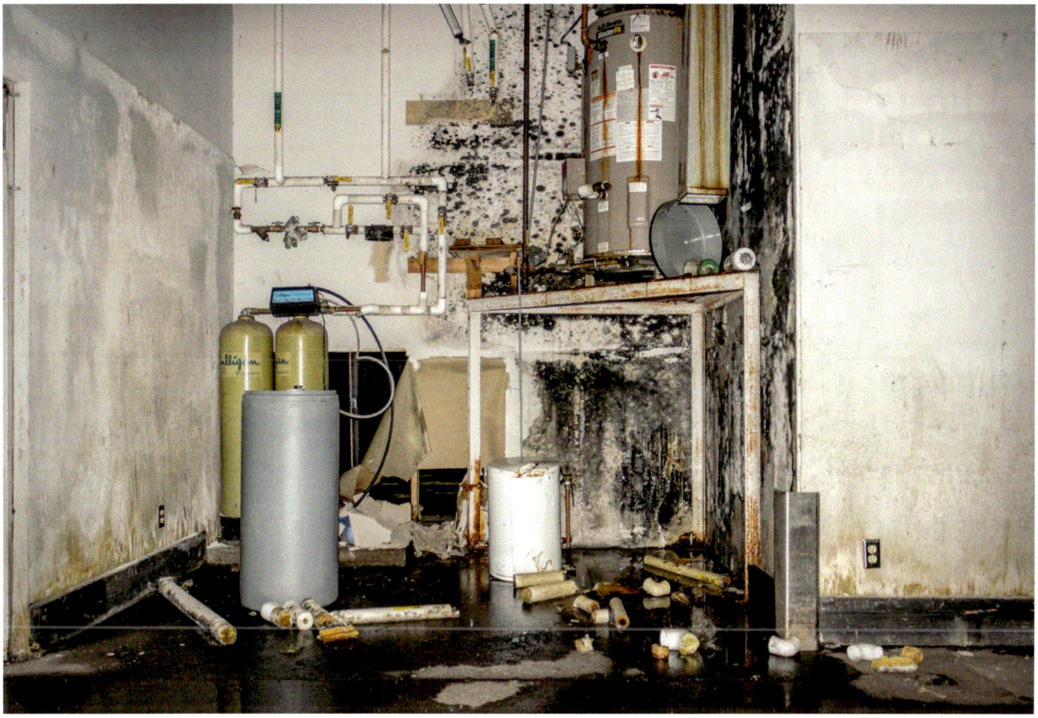

Corrosion and water damage produced a new home for black mold to settle into.

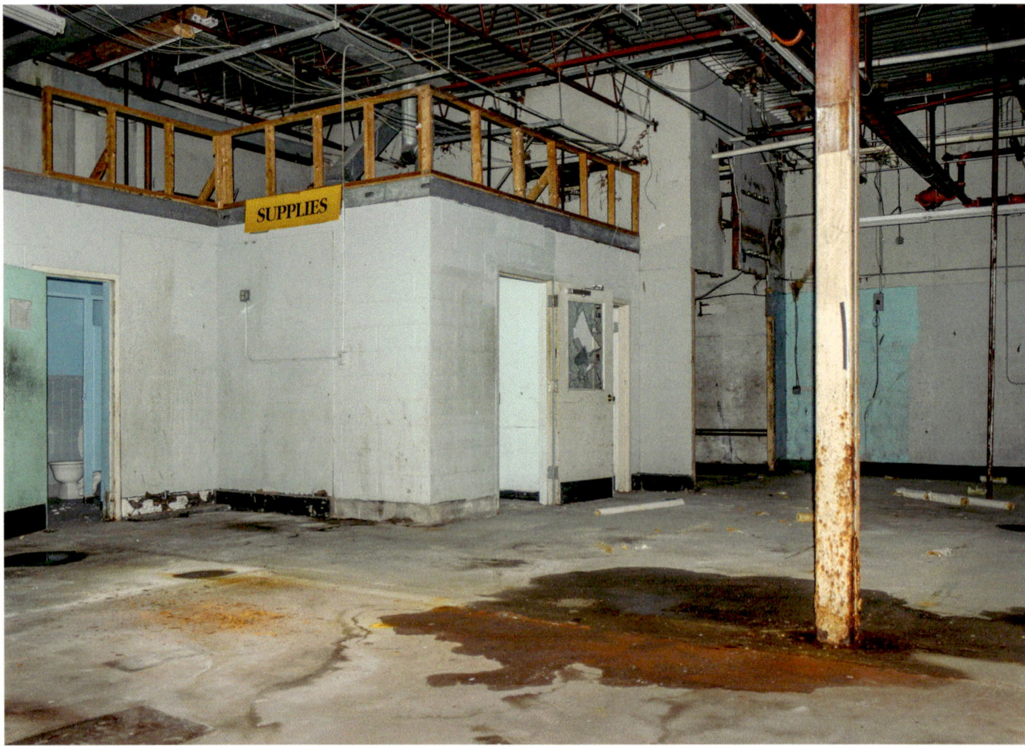

At the end of the hallway, a restroom and its neighboring supply room sit empty.

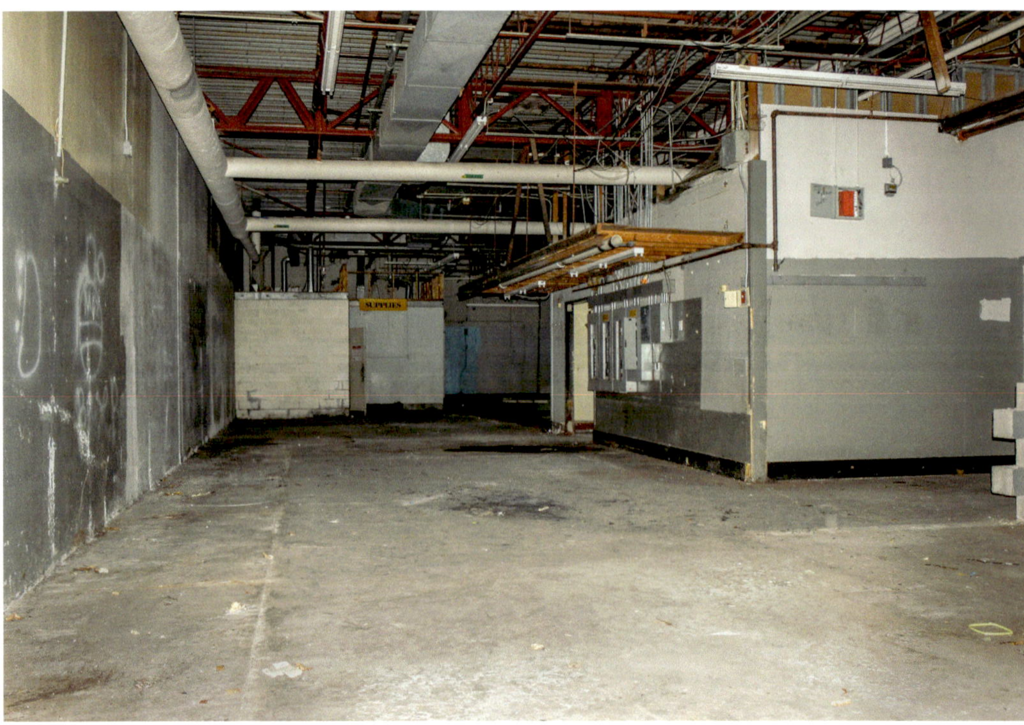

A right turn provides a view of the shell and its lack of debris and scraps.

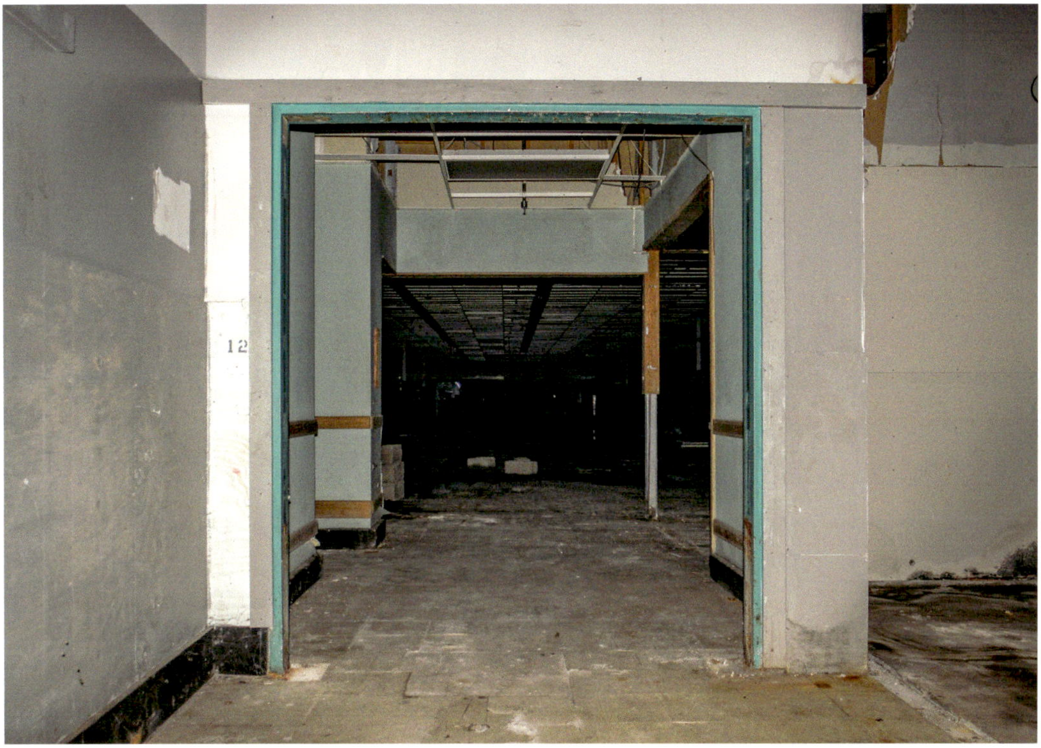

A doorway exposes a large opening to the heart of the building.

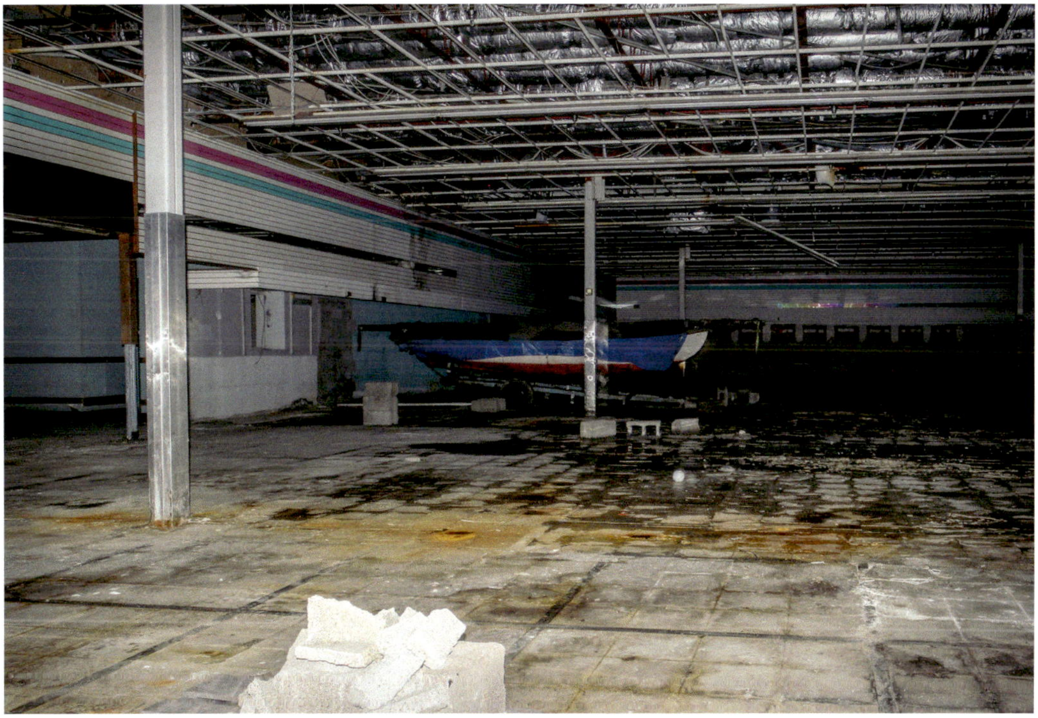

A boat, sheltered from the harsh upstate New York weather, patiently waits to see the light of day.

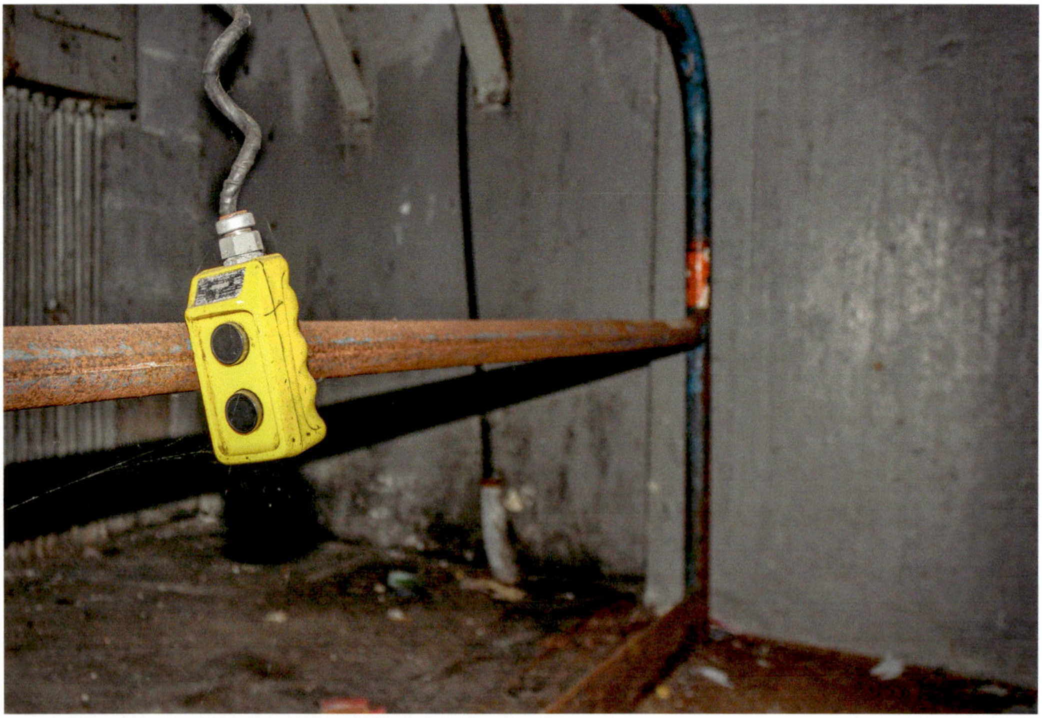

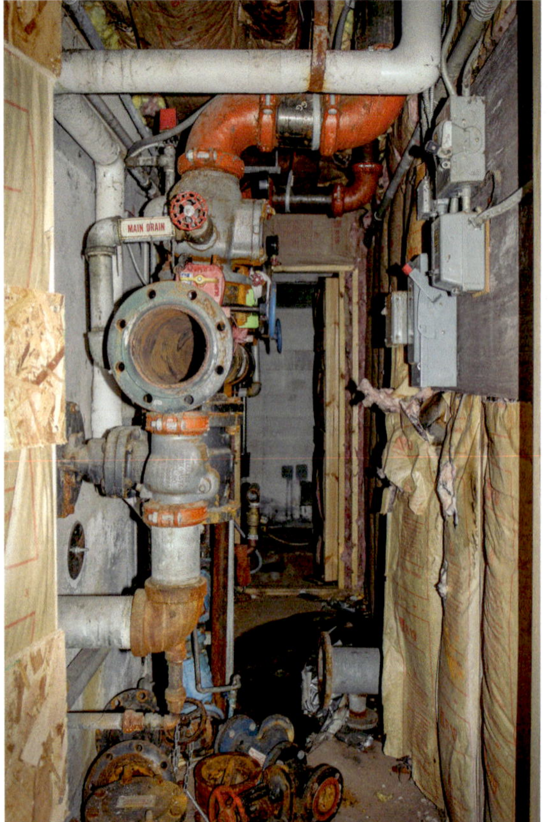

Above: A control switch dangles, helplessly, against the rusted structure of its lift.

Left: A maintenance closet left open, exposing the drainage system and pipes for the store.

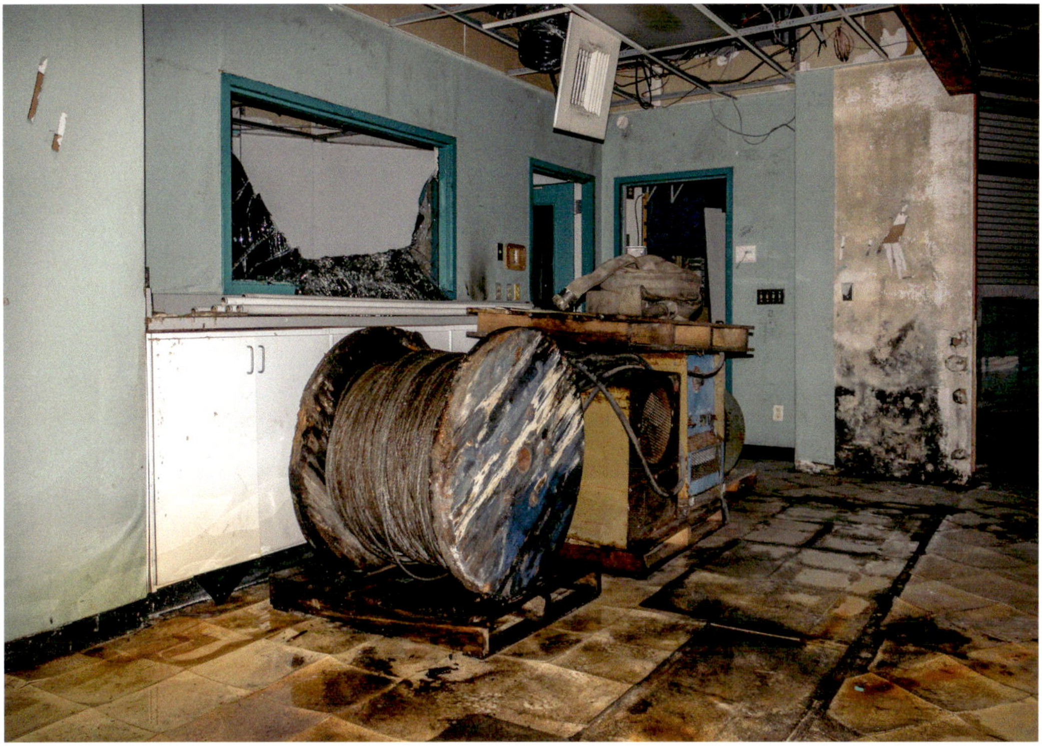

Resting outside a shattered window lies a large spool of cable, a water hose, and an obsolete ventilation system.

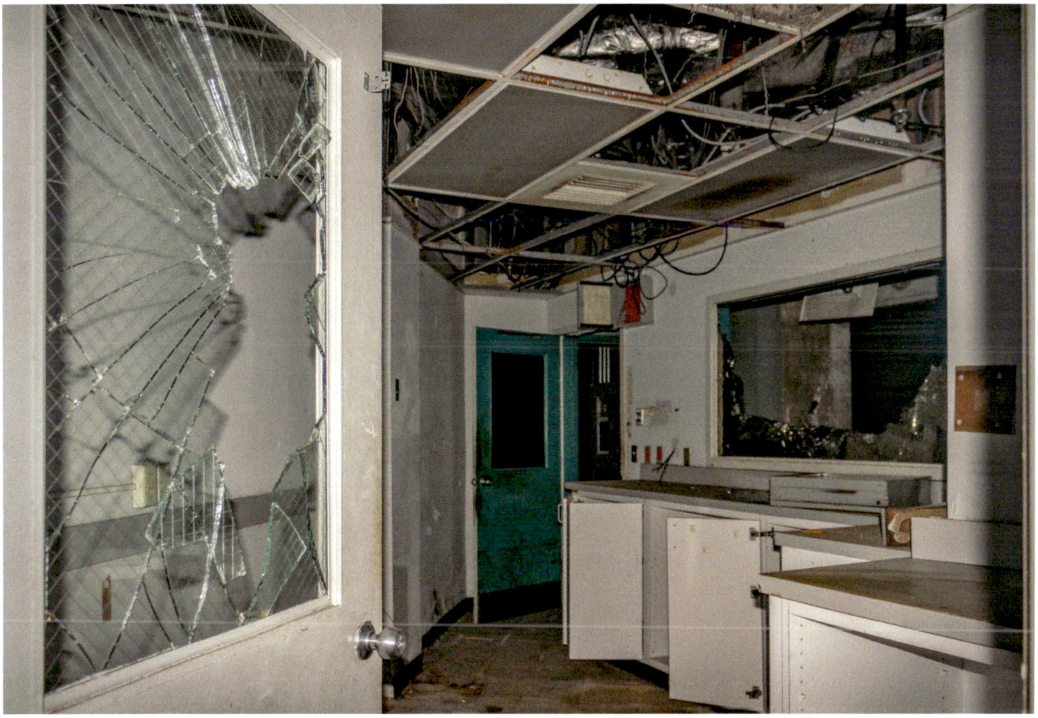

With distinct signs of forced entry, this room has fallen victim to thieves, searching through now-empty lockboxes.

7

READY-MIX CONCRETE PLANT

Active Dates Unknown

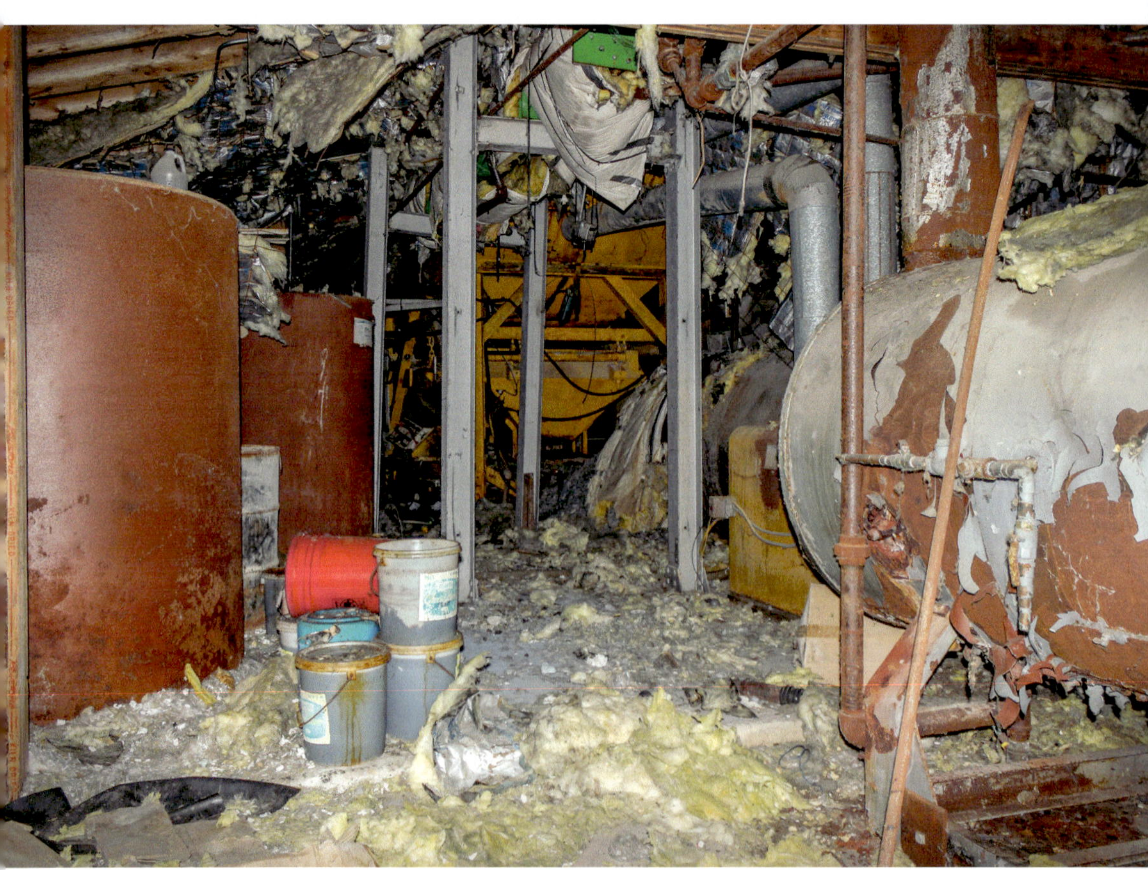

At first glance, many passersby would mistake this building for a house. I made the same mistake, until I entered the building. I made my way to the front of the house, in the dead of night; tall grass brushing against my knees. Once inside the threshold of the unlocked front door, I turned on my flashlight to see a large blue counter-top and remnants of shelving units, barely clinging to the walls. As I continued deeper through the structure, I arrived at a back doorway and was completely surprised to see three massive overgrown rooms. Collapsed sections of roofing and a hole in the floor had allowed the plants to bring life back into the rooms. Carefully stepping down broken stair planks, I followed a small stream of light leading me to a large board in the corner of the room. By brushing off years of dust and dirt, I was able to make out the words: "Ready-mix Concrete Plant." Now knowing the company name, I was on the hunt to find the machine/manufacturing room. I exited and walked around the right side of the building to find a staircase that lead to the second floor of the house. A faint shadow of a silo reared its face through the gaps in the staircase. Behind the silo, two additional building were camouflaged by nature. I entered one, turned on my flashlight, and found old, obsolete, machinery and decaying insulation covering the floor. Down a dark hallway decorated with equipment and old machines were used offices. The sensation of walking in the snow came over me as I trudged through insulation beneath my feet. Without my particle mask with a built-in respirator, this would have been detrimental to my health. Upon final inspection of the last office, I found stacked boxes hidden behind a wall, which contained everything from order forms and purchase receipts to clientele lists and invoices. With more than enough photos and history of the Ready-mix Concrete Plant, I headed home.

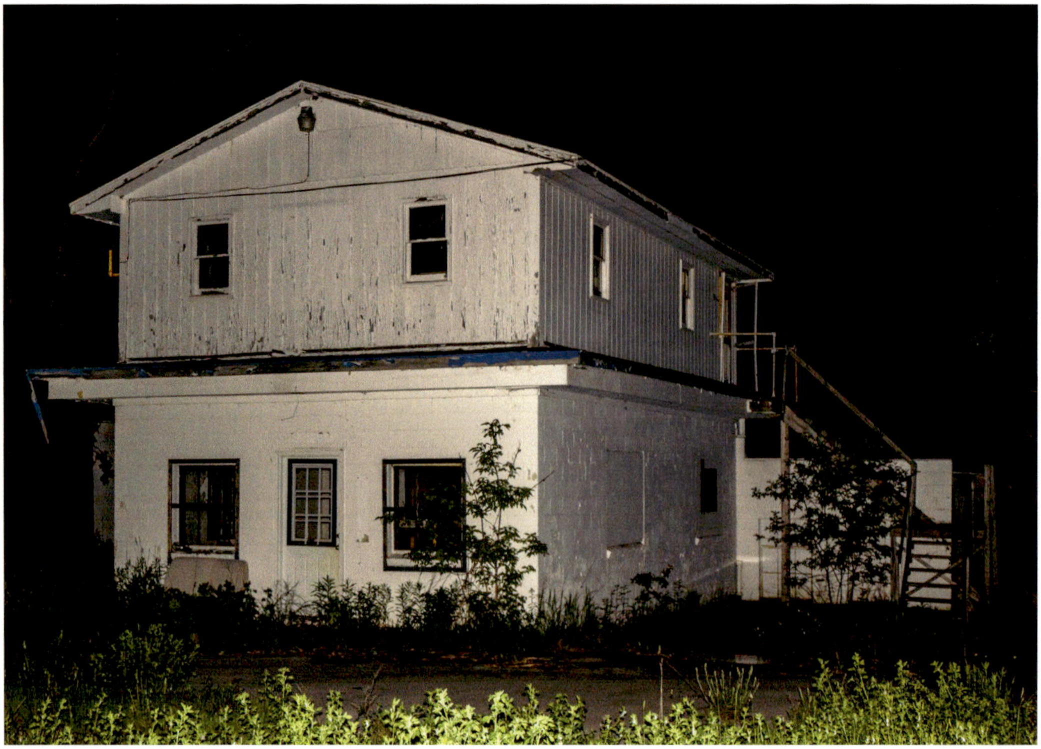

Hidden in the shadows lies the entrance of the concrete plant.

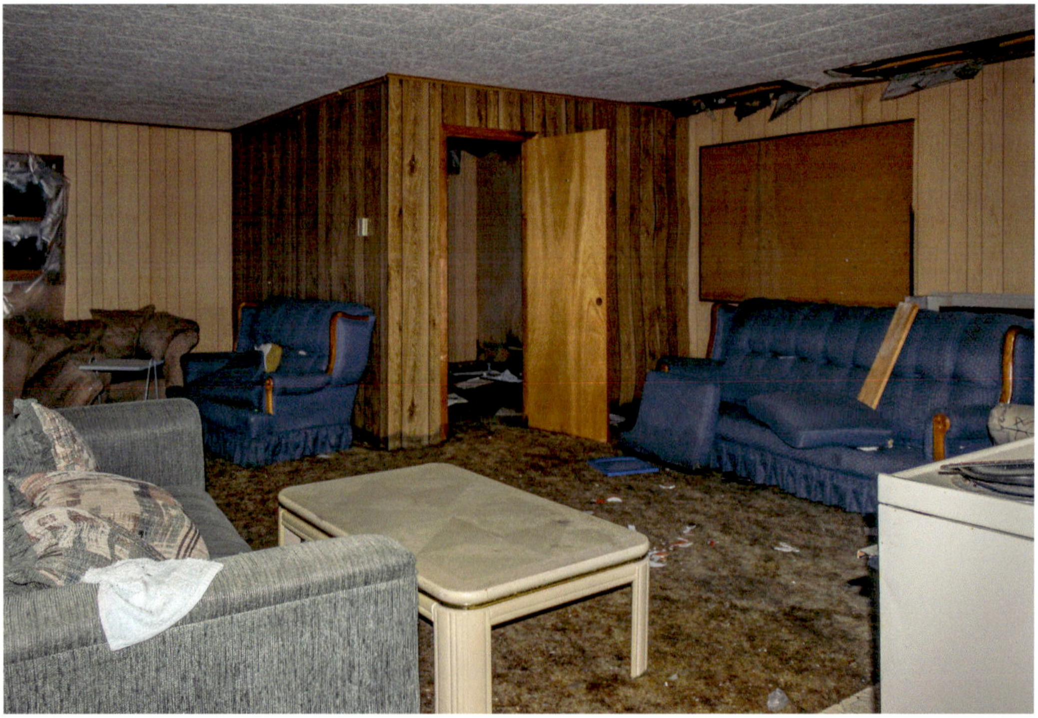

The second-floor employee lounge.

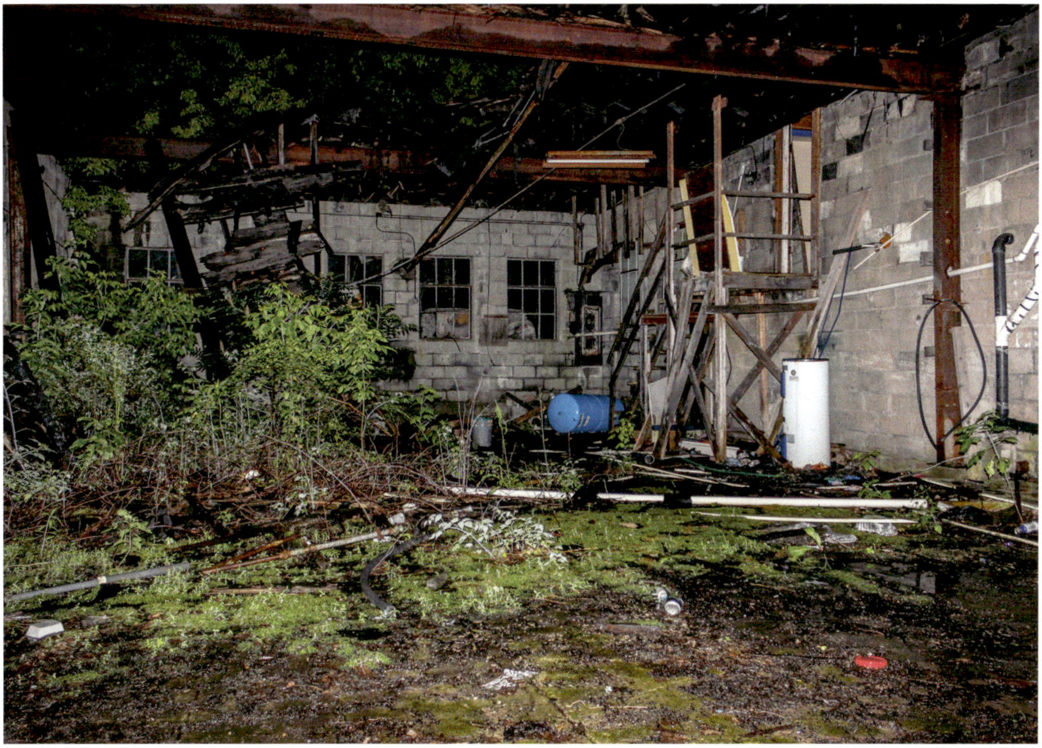

The entrance to the first garage, littered with debris and plant life.

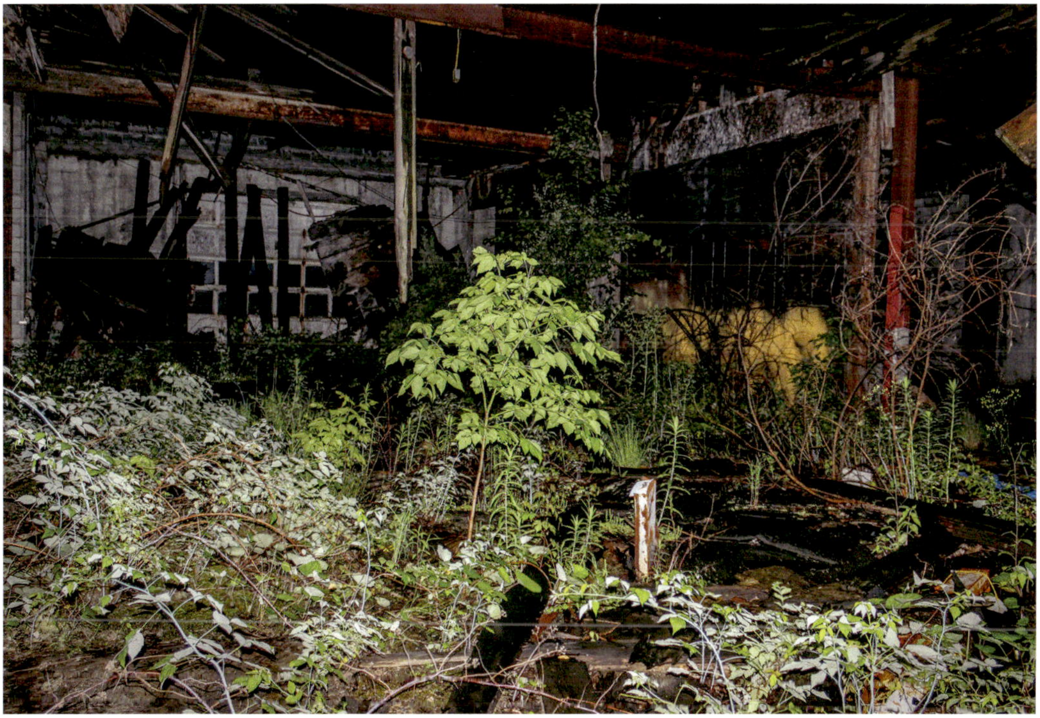

The remains of the second garage, completely engulfed in foliage.

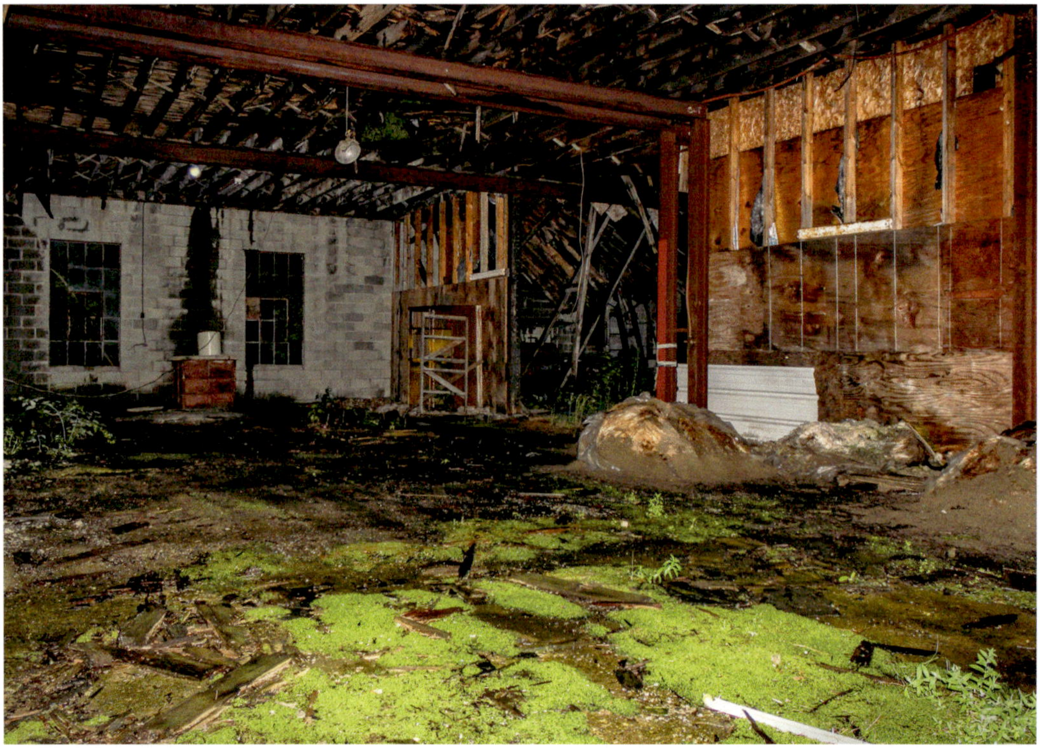

The third garage seems to have been spared from natures' consumption.

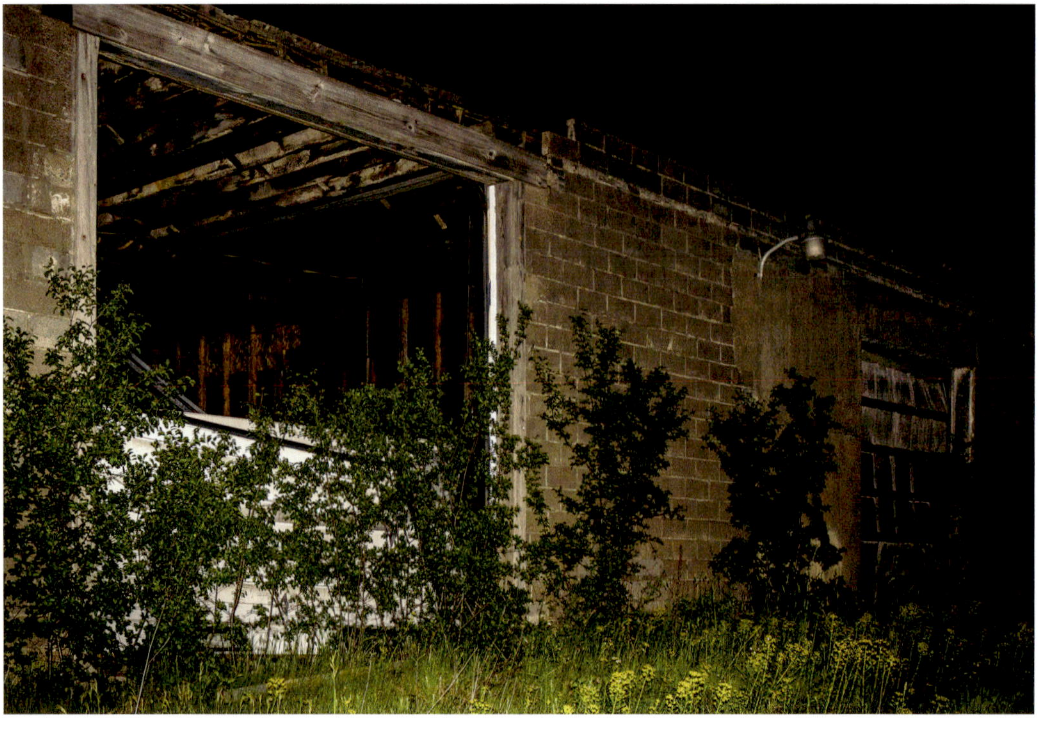

An exterior glimpse of the first two garage doors, as I made my way to the last building extension.

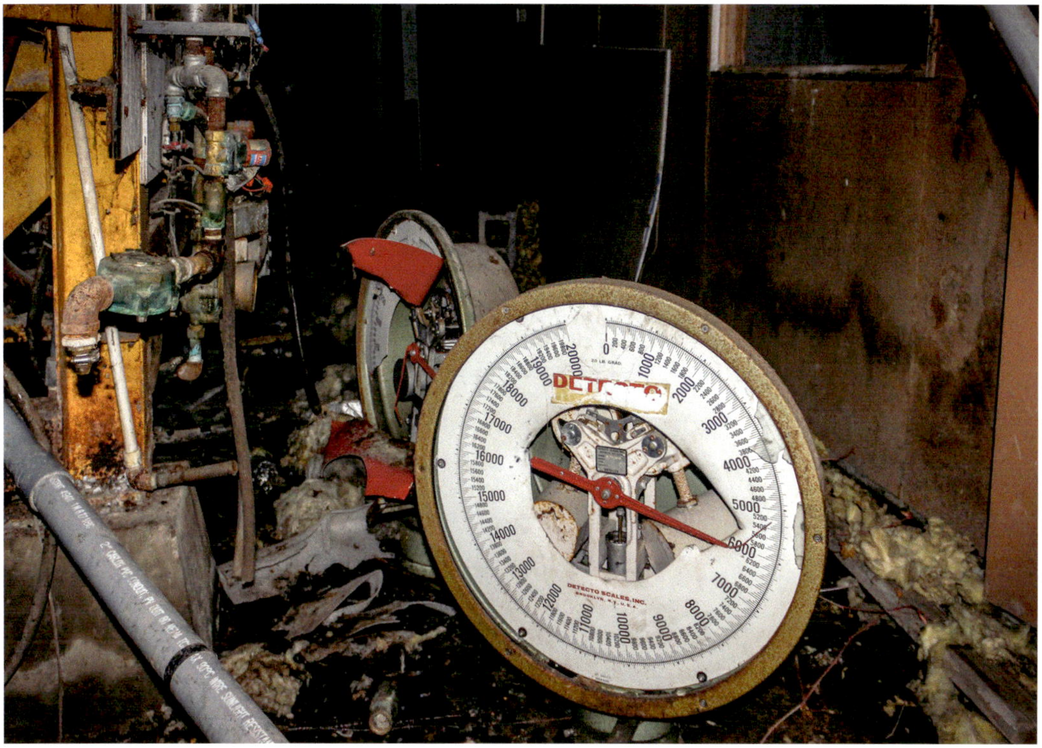

A destroyed scale shows us the vast amount of material that was created at this plant.

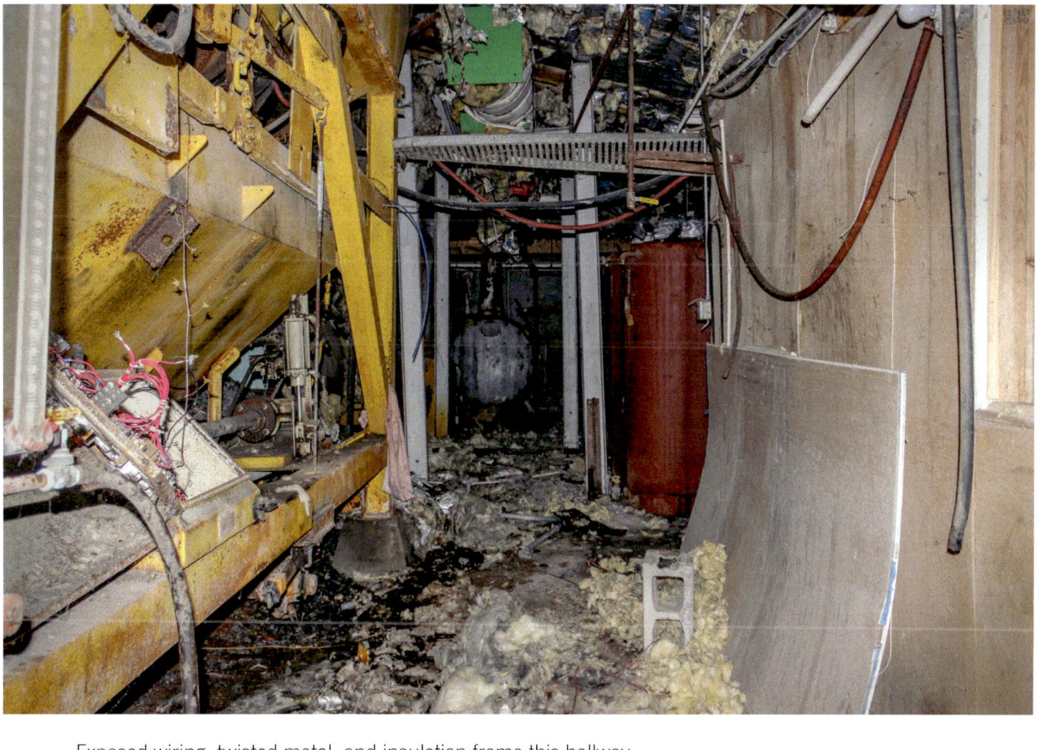

Exposed wiring, twisted metal, and insulation frame this hallway.

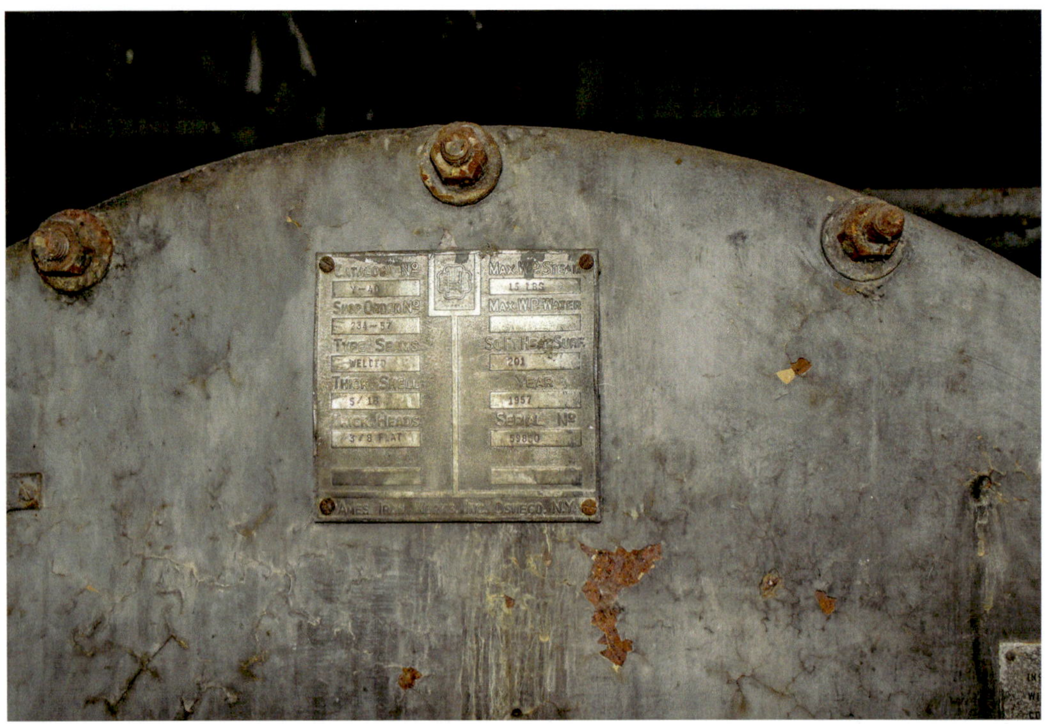

The date on the plate in this pressure chamber gives us a rough idea of when this plant began production.

8

HOUSE ON RT. 49

Active Dates Unknown

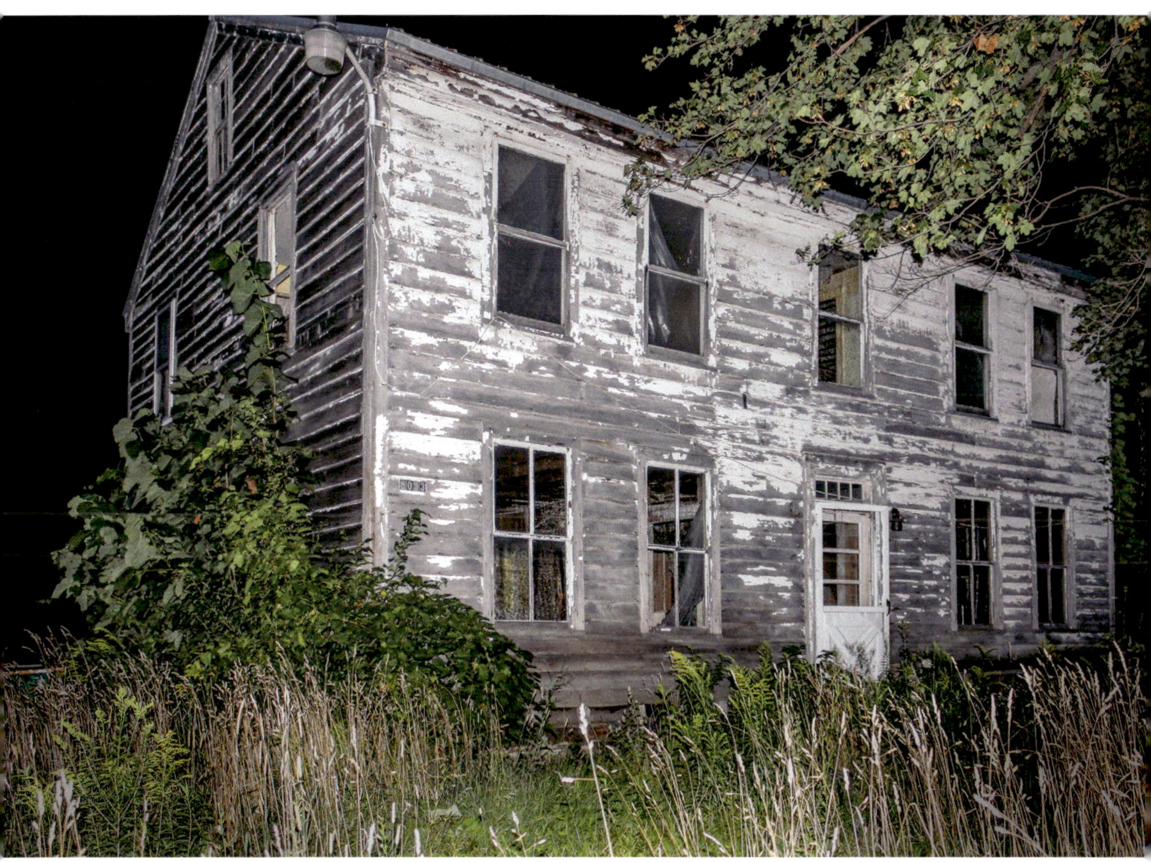

I discovered this house while driving to an abandoned paper mill. With a small change of plans, I parked my car, grabbed my flashlight and camera, and began scoping out the perimeter of the house. I opened the front door and went in. Aware of surrounding neighbors, I used my flashlight sparingly. As I felt my way through the first room, I was hit face-first with a soft mesh feel. I shined my light and saw a large artificial spider web, set up for Halloween. There were fake severed limbs, mannequins in costume, plastic pumpkins, and skulls huddled in corners; I had just walked into an old mock-haunted house. This discovery downstairs eased my level of concern as I headed up the stairs to a scene of splattered blood all over the walls. The rest of the upstairs was minimally decorated with some empty rooms and some stacked with furniture and discarded household items. After investigating the upstairs, I went back down to the kitchen where I had remembered seeing a shut door. This was the door to the basement. Opening the door, I ventured down the broken stairs, my flashlight beaming through the airborne dust and particles. The smell of mold surrounded my respirator. Leaves from the open cellar door littered the surface of the floor. There was not much more to see but some obsolete equipment caked in debris. I made my way out and resumed my original course to the abandoned mill.

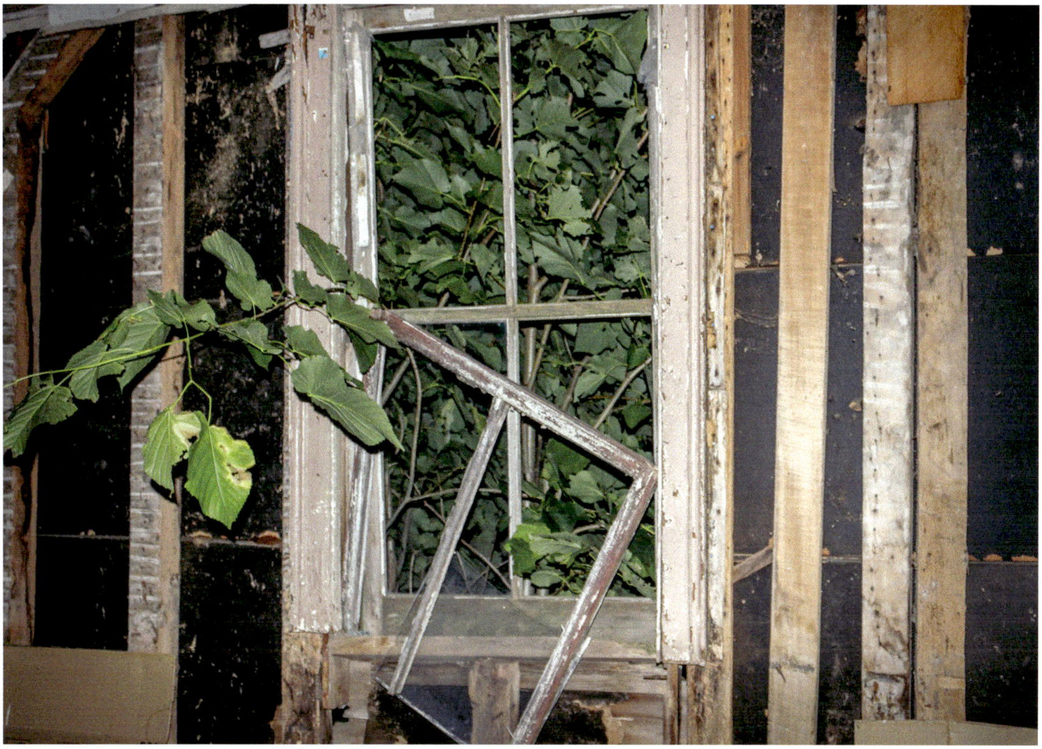

A thin sapling branch finds opportunity through a broken windowpane.

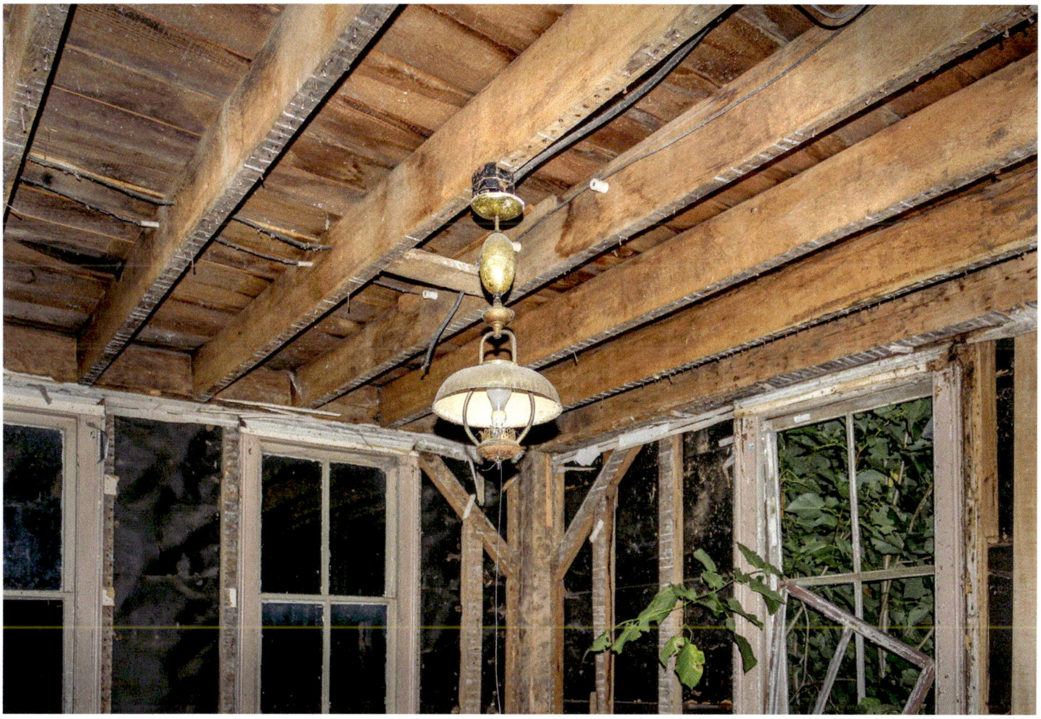

A step back from the window reveals an old light dangling from the ceiling.

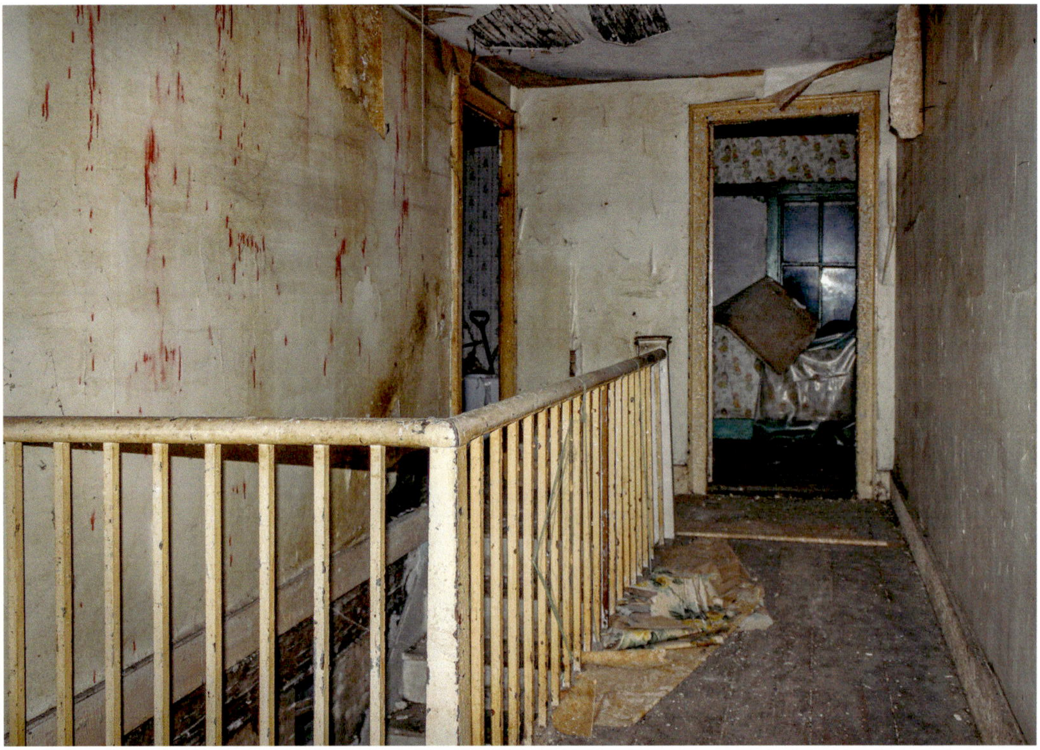

The staircase, painted in a mock horror scene, splattered with fake blood.

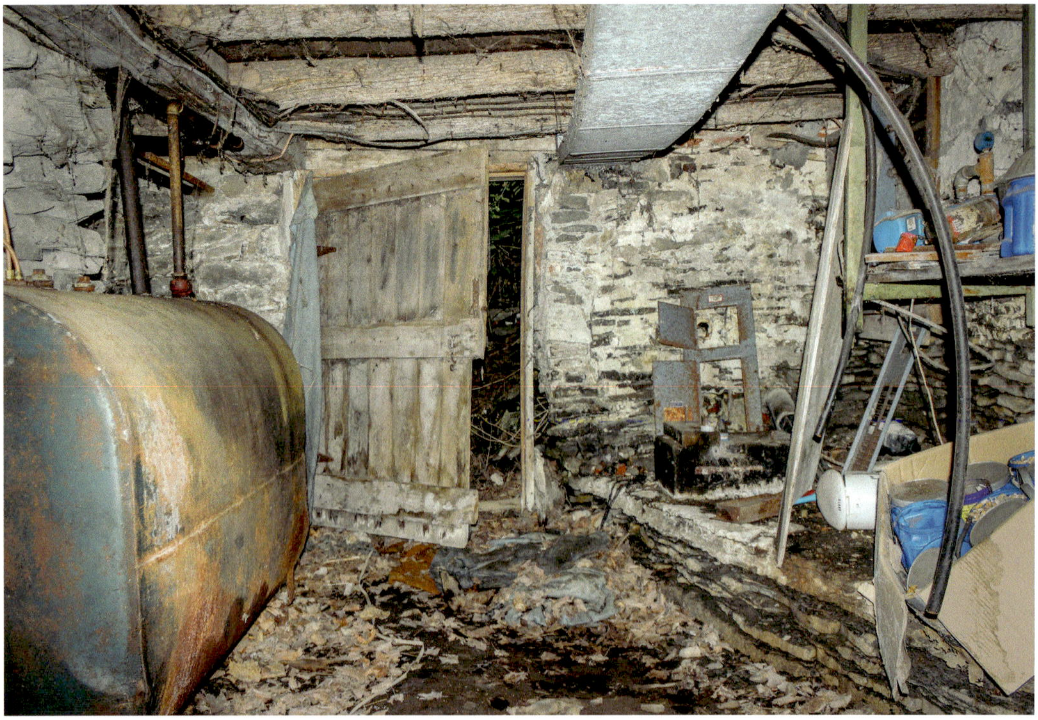

One last photo before heading out the cellar door of the basement.

9

SECOND HOUSE ON RT. 49

ACTIVE DATES UNKNOWN

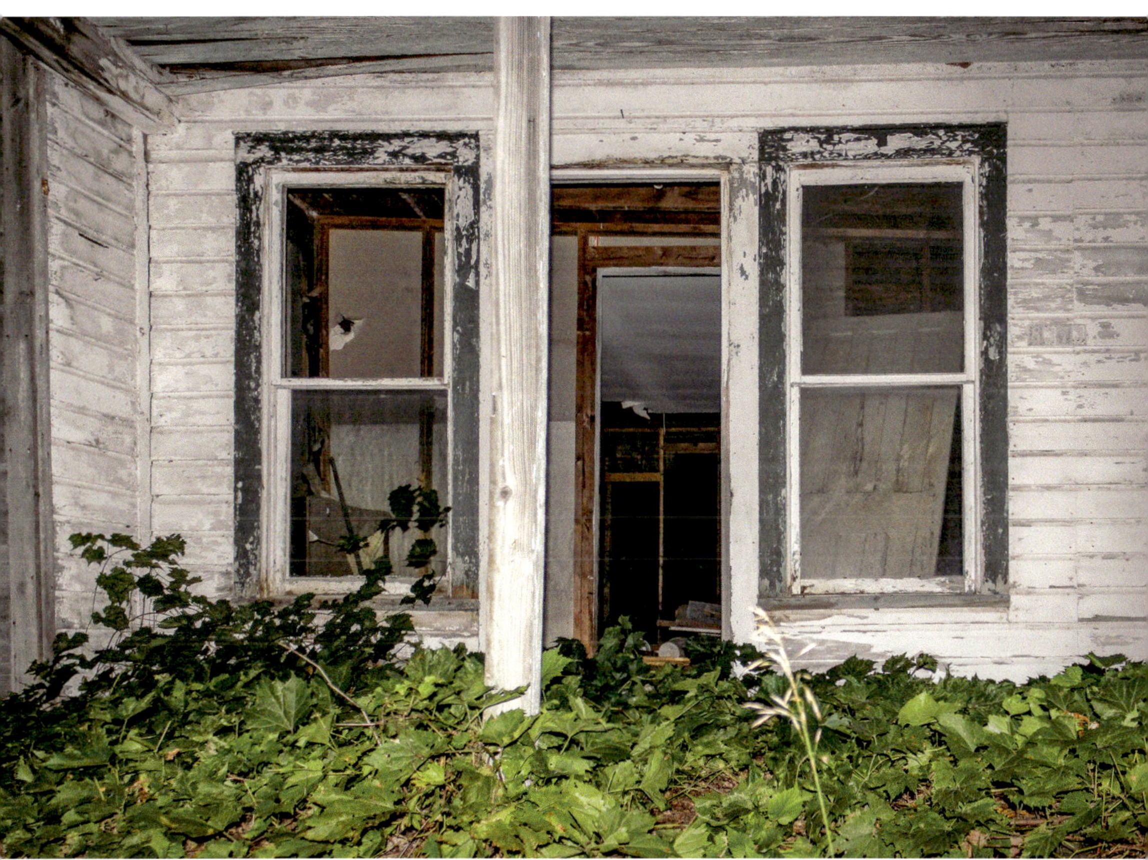

After my brief detour of the Halloween house, I continued down the same road. The woods grew thicker as I traveled further down the winding road. A reflection to my left revealed a shattered window hiding in the tree line. I pulled over and grabbed my camera. The woods were thick with saplings and grass taller than me. There were many times during this short hike that I began to question if the glare was real or just my imagination. I pressed further and finally came to a house with an appearance straight out of a horror film. This house was the most dilapidated building I had ever explored. The porch was entirely engulfed with vines and brush. My first step onto the porch resulted in my foot passing right through the plank and onto the ground. It was a good thing this porch was only a foot or two off the ground. Marching my way through the vines, I made it into the house and found the floor completely absent, with only the bare foundation remaining. Meticulously placing each step, I made my way to the downstairs. As if the appearance and location wasn't creepy enough, I discovered an old well in the basement of the house. I had never imagined I would see a house with a well in the basement outside of horror movies, but this house proved me wrong. After taking some photos of the basement and shell of the house, I made my way towards the more feasible storm door exit in the basement. Although the house was mostly degraded and bare, the experience was worth the hike through the thick woods. It was now going on 2:00 a.m., and these houses had distracted me from the intended trip to the paper mill; I would have to plan on visiting another time.

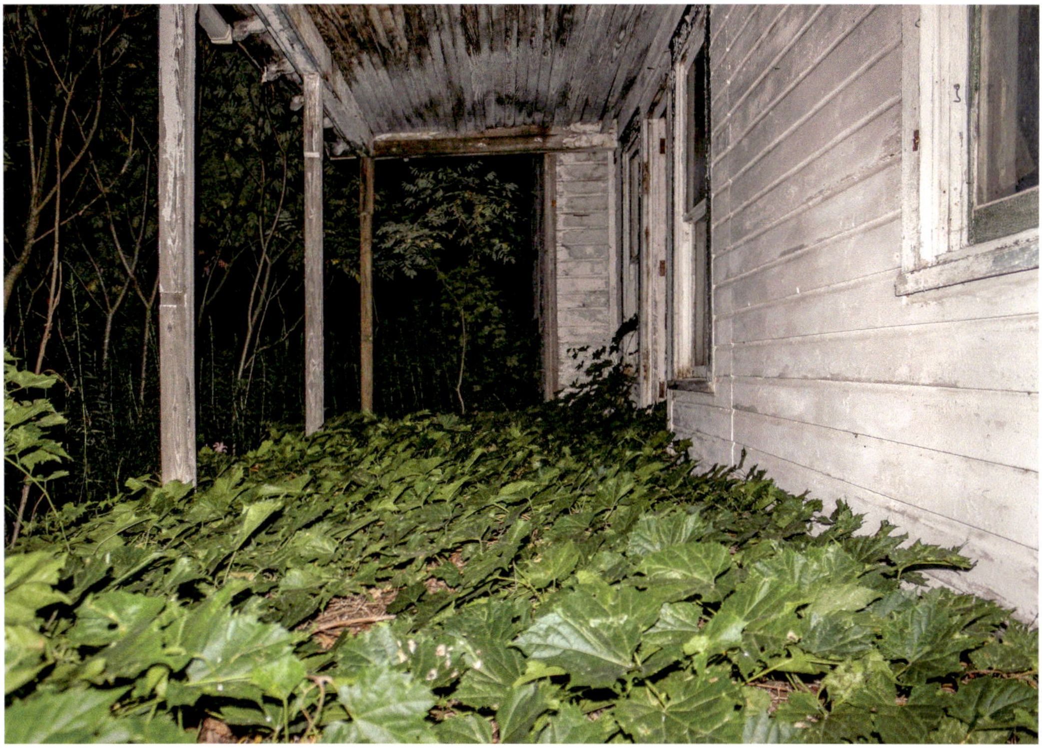

Walking up to the house, a glimpse down the overgrown porch.

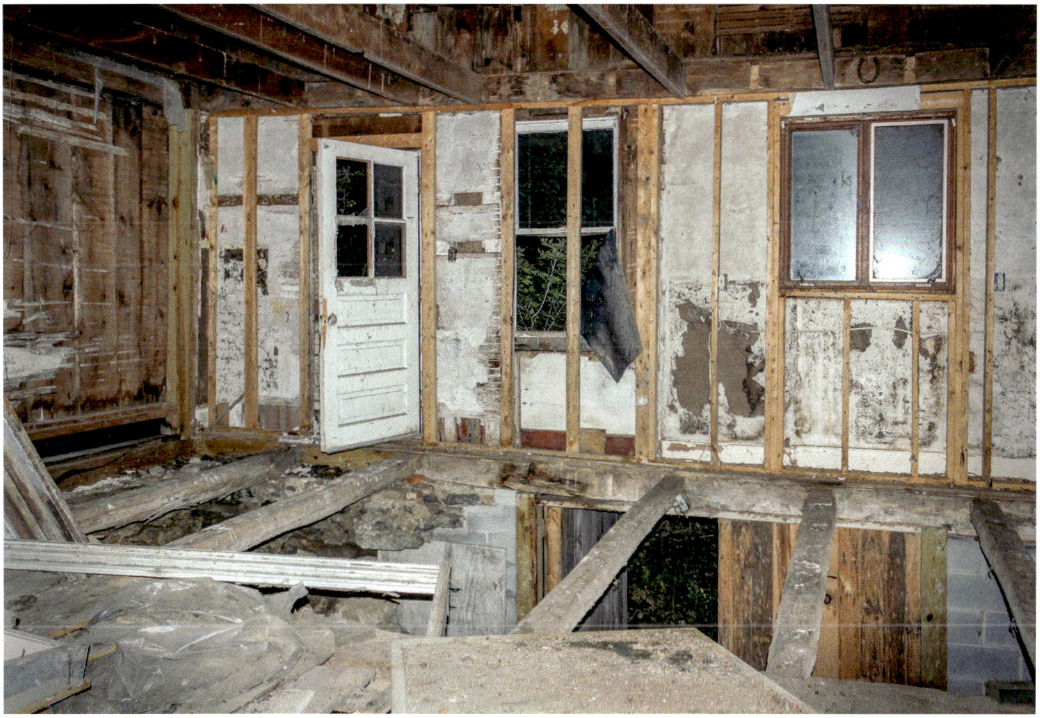

All that remains of this interior is a few intact windows, and some floor foundation.

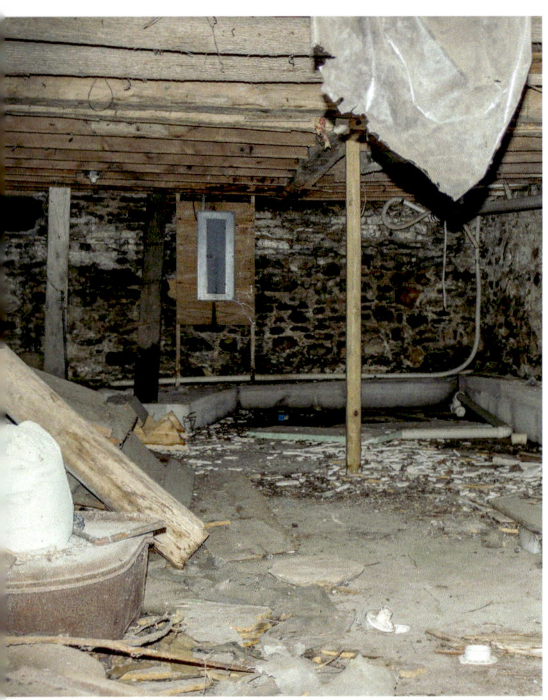

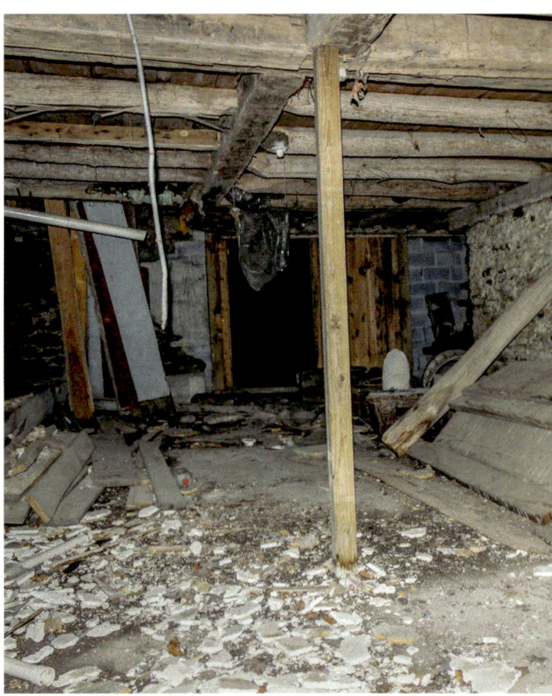

Above left: Finding my way down to the basement, I begin to feel more and more like a horror movie protagonist.

Above right: A shot facing away from the well, with the storm door exit in sight.

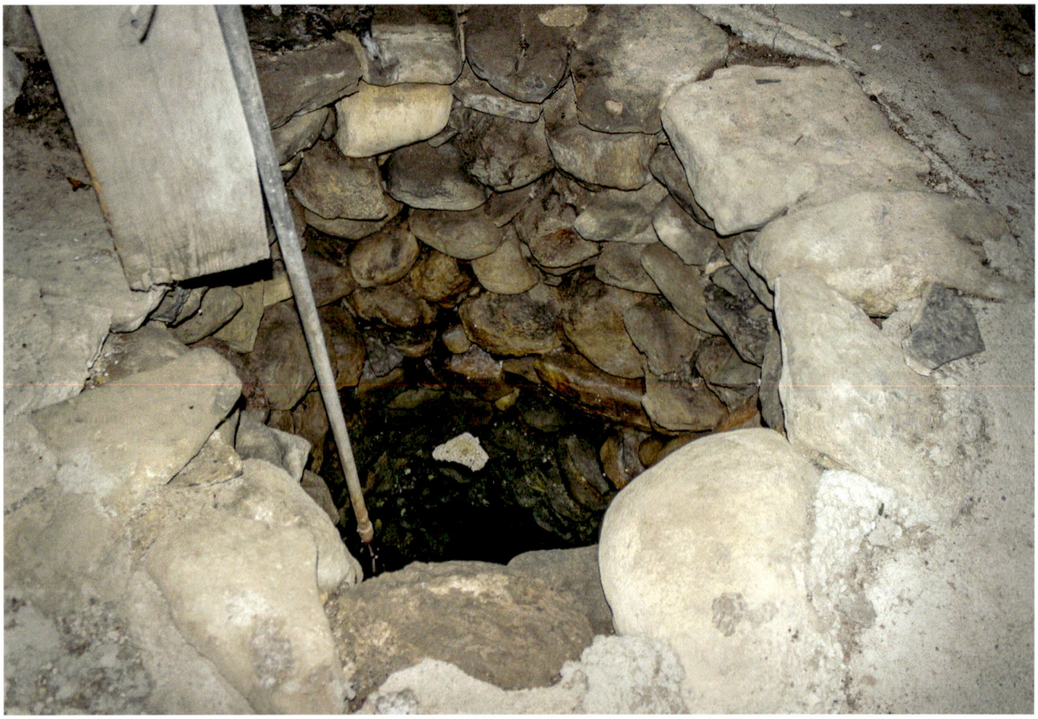

A look down the well that lies in the far corner of the basement.

10

HOUSE ON RT. 59

Active Dates Unknown

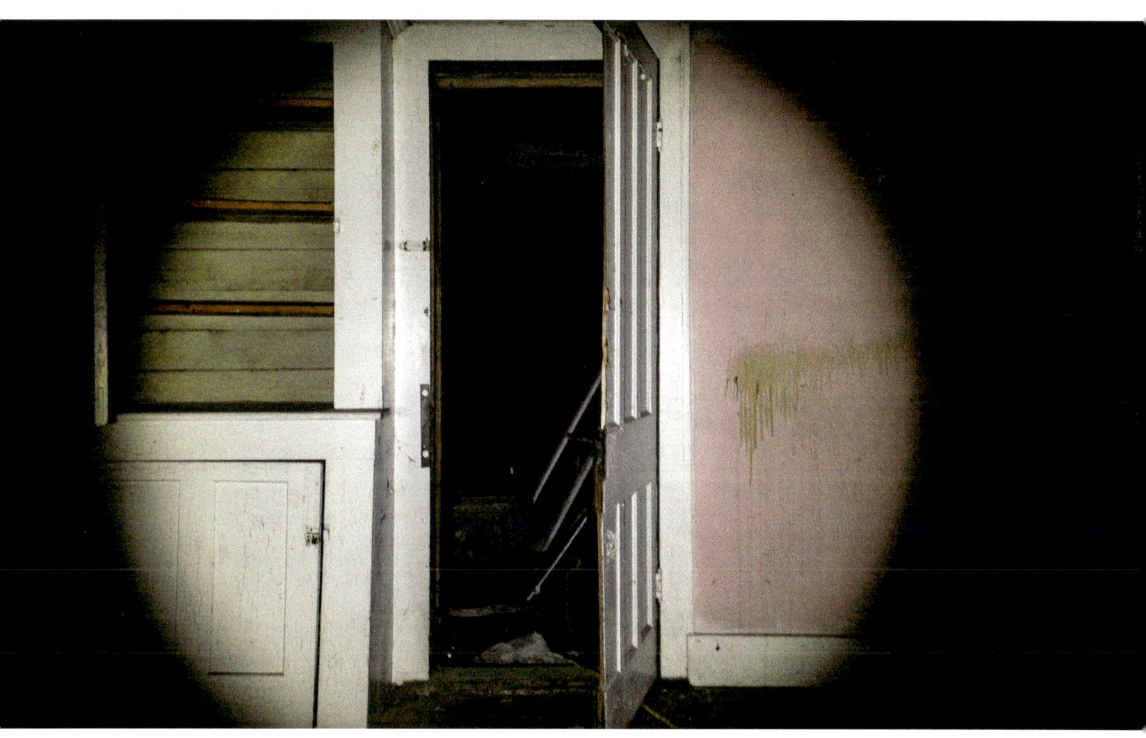

One of the most difficult explorations I have done is this house. It sits a few feet from a busy highway. Time of day did not work to my advantage. It was 3:00 a.m. and the road was still busy with traffic. I had to use my camera flash and flashlight sparingly so I did not to bring attention to my investigation. I found a secluded spot to park my car, and then blindly crept through the tall grass to the back door of the house. I sat still and listened for the sound of cars to make sure I was alone and able to turn on my flashlight. With the background noise of tires fading, I turned on my flashlight and found myself in the kitchen. Unfortunately, I had to change my plans when the sound of a car seemed to come close to the house. I had to navigate myself around the first floor in complete darkness. I managed to find my way into one of the first-floor bedrooms. Once the street sounds faded, I turned on my light and was greeted by an old bed and record player cabinet. The woodwork and condition of the record player was astoundingly pristine. My admiration was short lived by another approaching car; back to complete darkness. Peeled layers of wallpaper lightly rubbed against my fingers as I used them to guide me from room to room. When I was again able to turn on my light, I discovered an intimidating basement door. I scurried down the steps into a typical unfinished basement layout. Decaying water heaters, rusted air ducts, and dusty shelves were all this basement had to offer. As I headed back upstairs, I turned off my light and maneuvered my way to the second floor. Using my camera, I snapped a few photos and made use of the light from the flash to be my guide to the attic. The attic was cleaned out with not a single item left behind. This is very rare for abandoned houses. I took one more photo, then I muted my lights and headed out to the garage. Not finding a visible entrance to the garage, I poked my camera through a shattered windowpane and took a photo. The flash illuminated an old John Deere tractor, which had been there for many years. It sat, no longer able to be ridden, coated with generous amounts of rust and tire rot.

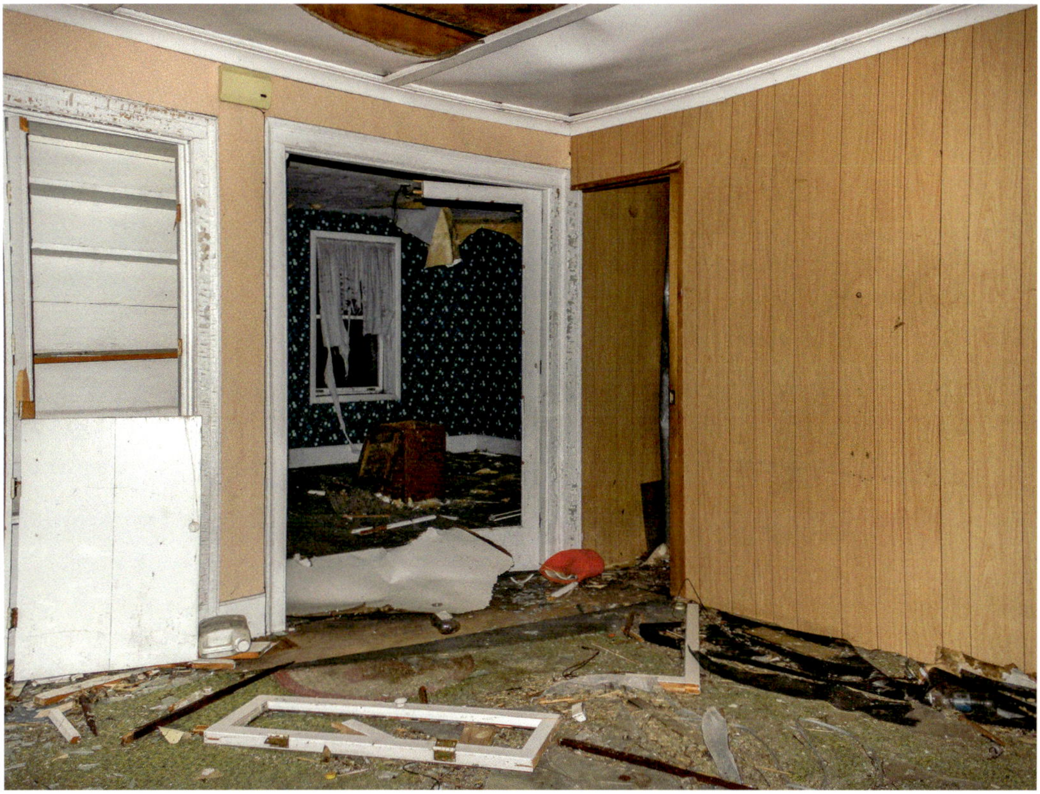

The living room waits helplessly with its cabinets ripped open and glass shards strewn across the floor.

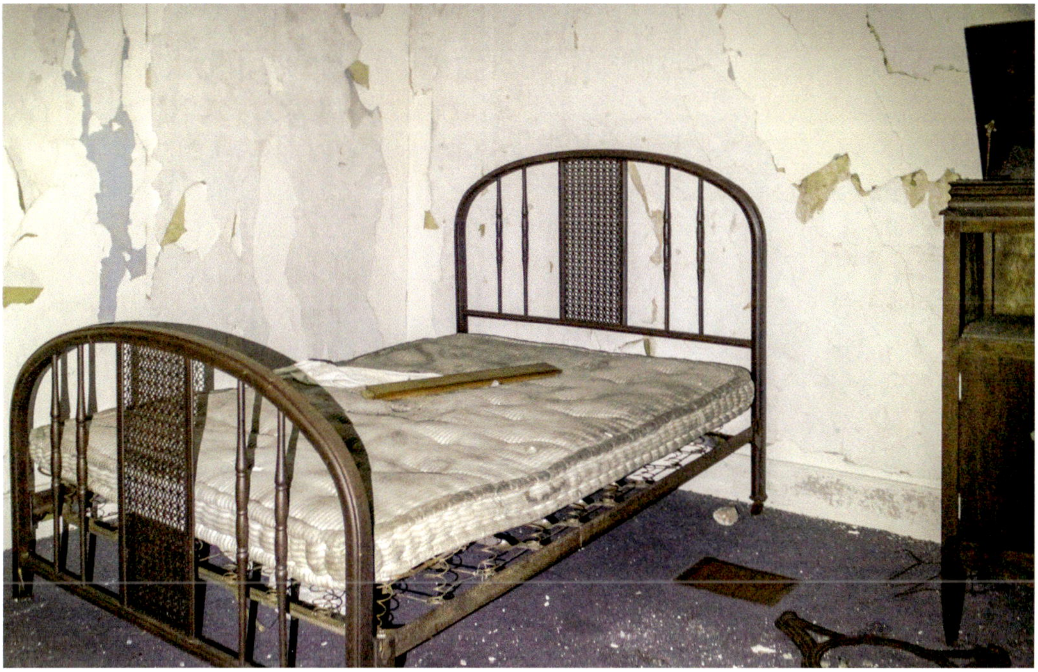

An old spring bedframe and an antique record player.

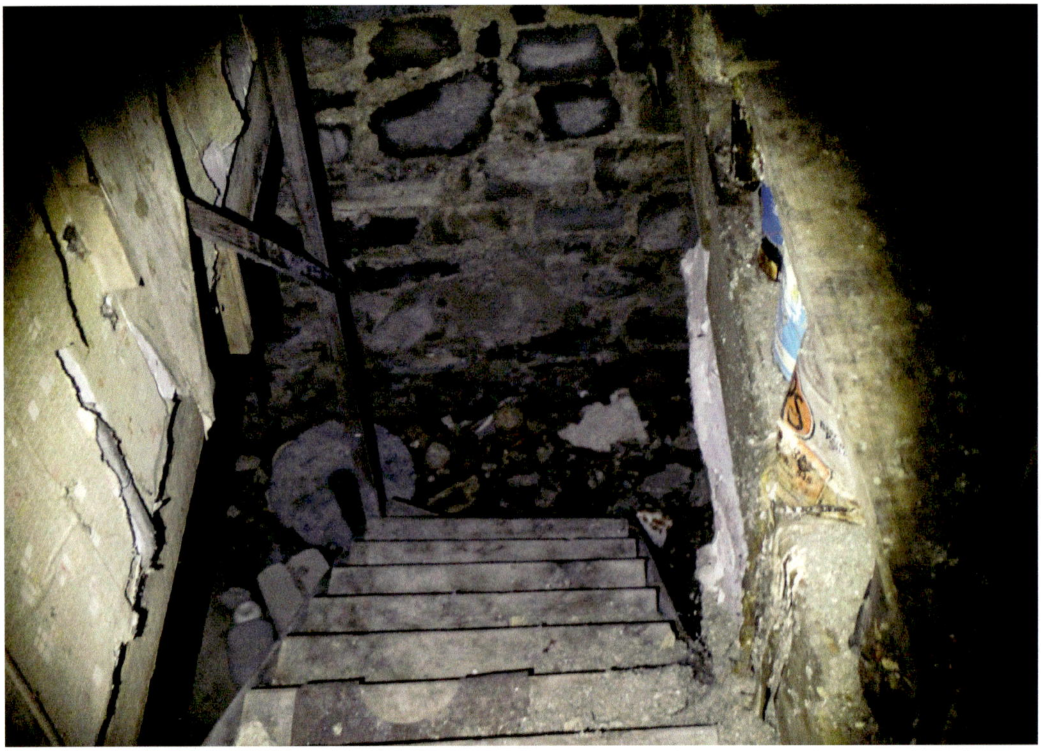

A view down into the basement.

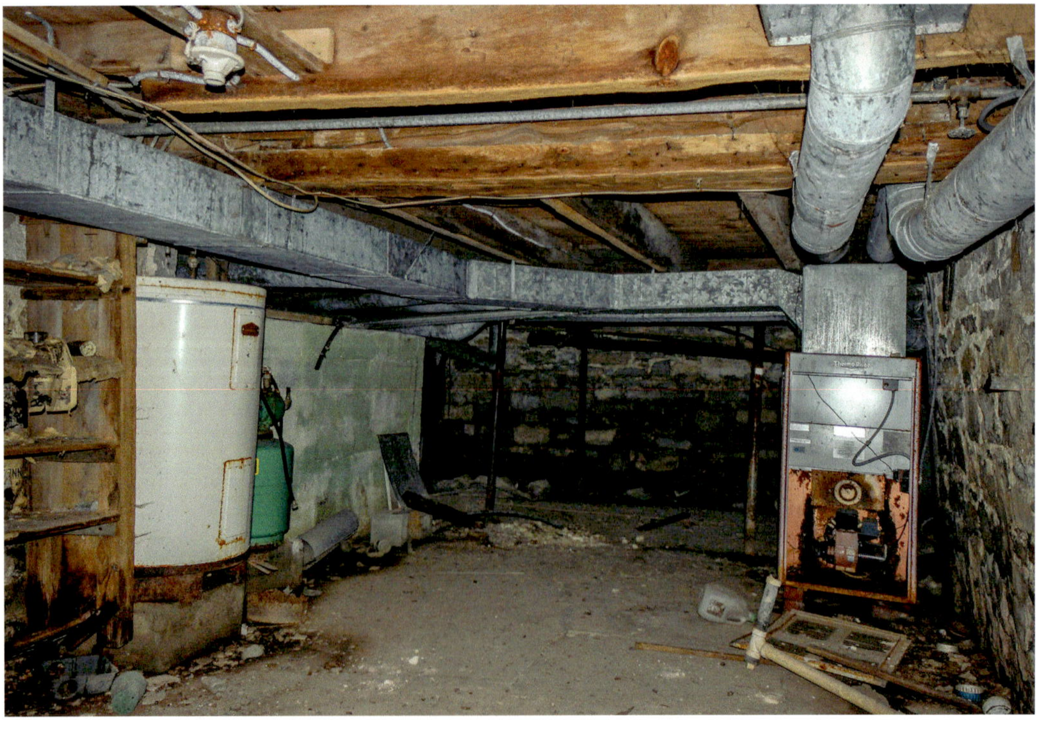

In the basement, air ducts hang as contaminated water trickles down the stone foundation.

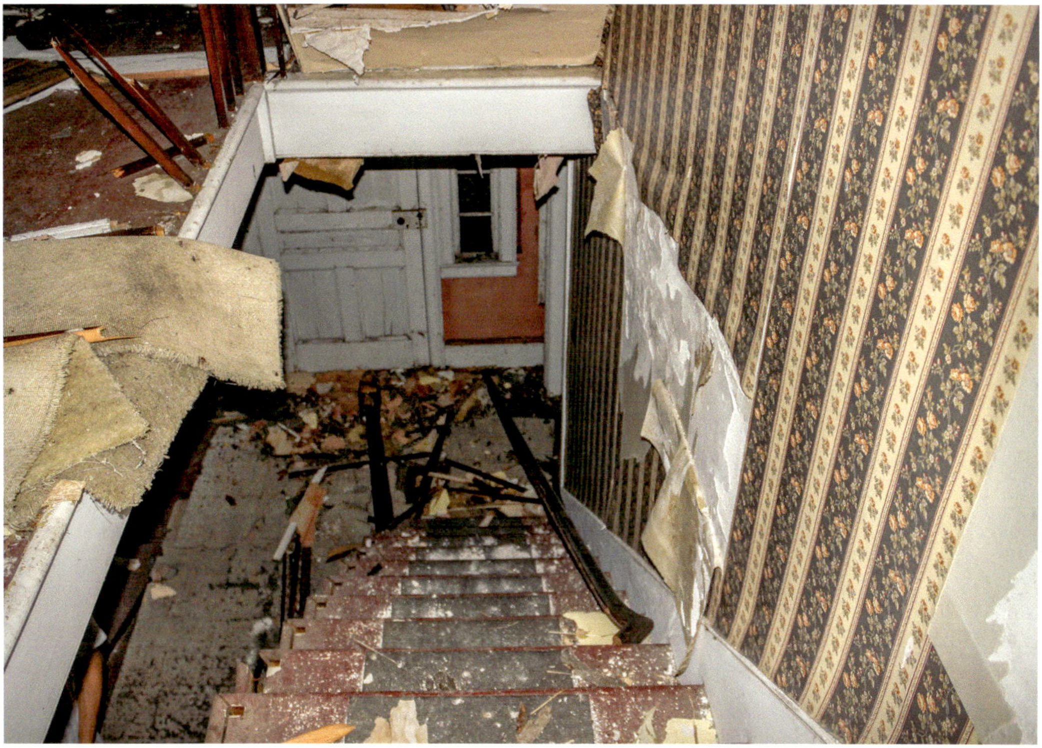

Fractured pieces of wood railings and paneling lie across the staircase.

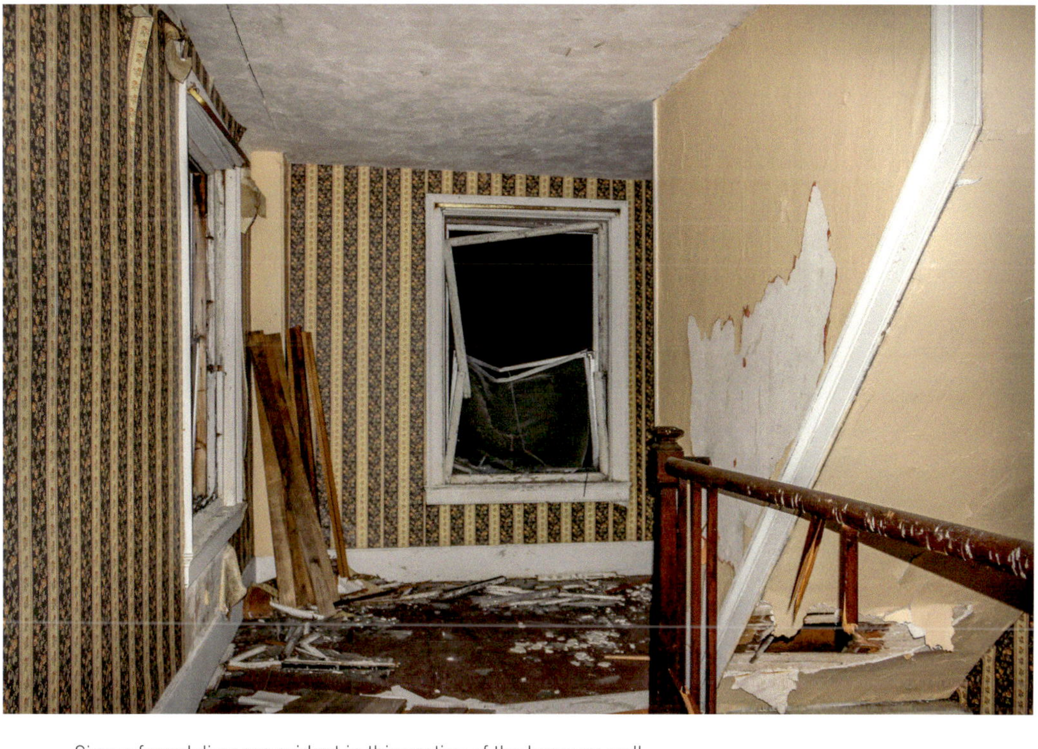

Signs of vandalism are evident in this section of the home as well.

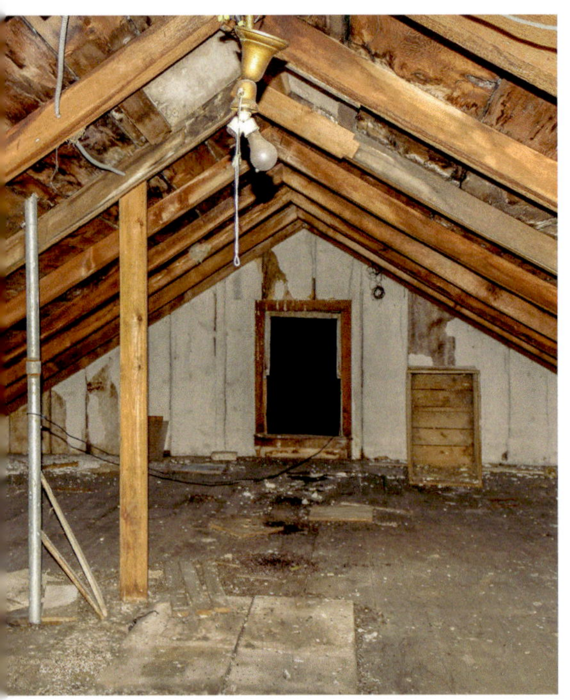

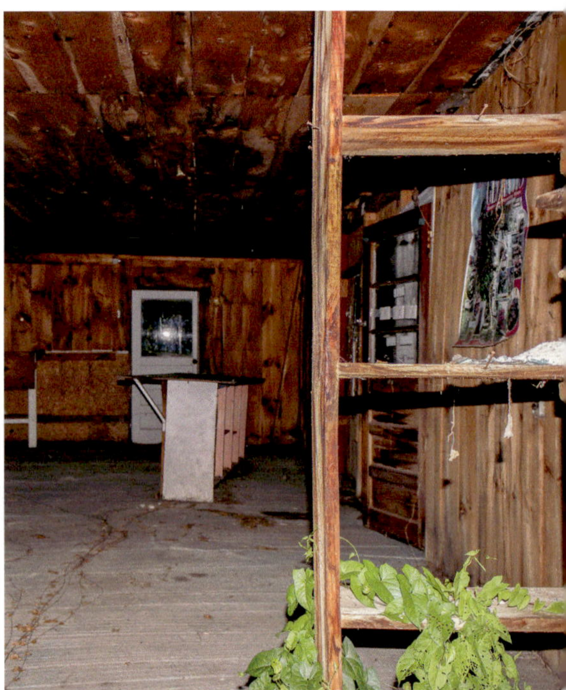

Above left: A bare attic provides refuge for bats and other curious animals.

Above right: A storage room sits empty next to the garage.

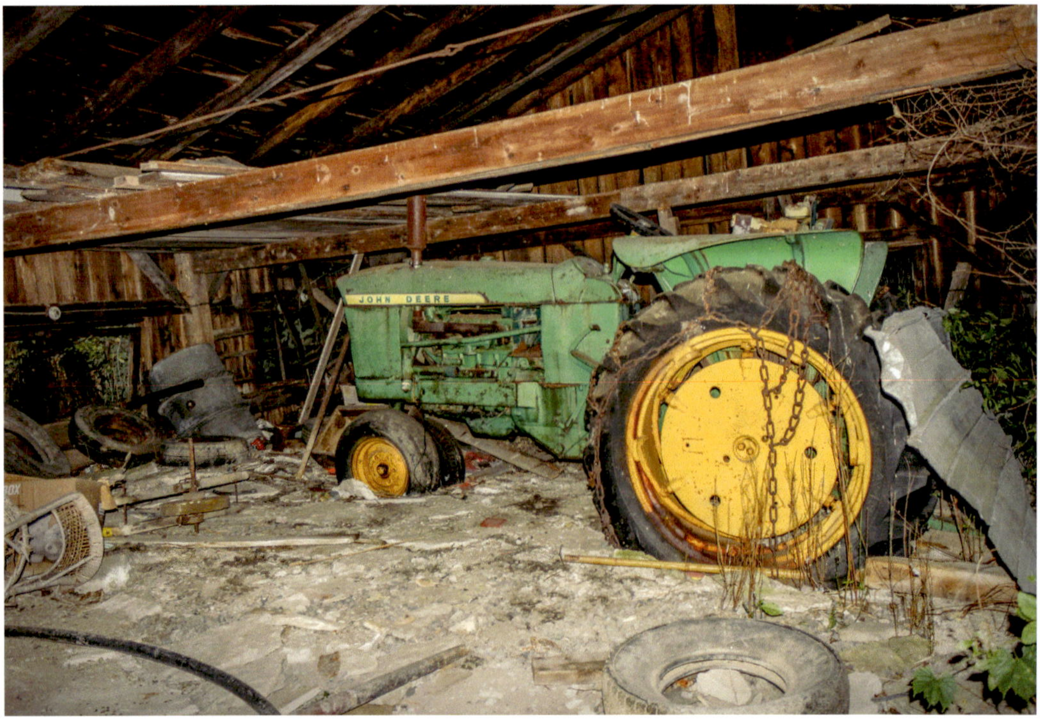

Poor old John Deere sits waiting among other deteriorated outdoor equipment.

11

HOUSE ON RT. 81

Active Dates Unknown

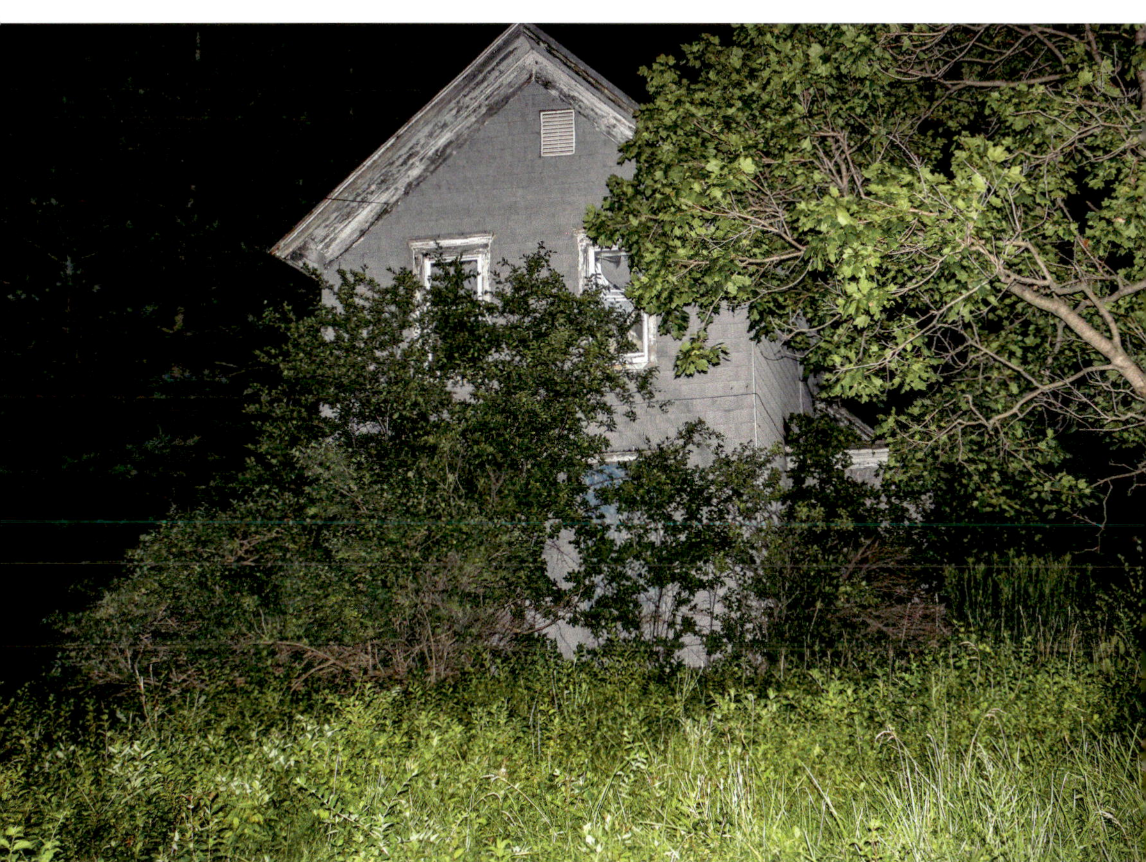

Concealed from plain sight by an array of trees and shrubs, this house has fallen victim to an obscene amount of vandalism. The back doorway's glass was shattered, evidence of a previous forced entry. Glass and plastic crunched under my feet as I entered the house. A crude path, littered with cabinet doors, boxes, and household items was what I followed throughout my exploration of the house. In the kitchen, appliances and cabinets were ripped off the walls, and discarded goods and utensils were strewn around what was once the kitchen. As I made my way into the living room, the destruction of the interior seemed to increase. I continued upstairs finding even more belongings smashed and neglected. A sense of sorrow grew within me as I witnessed the aftermath of a family's memories, ripped apart with each room I entered. Shattered family photos, aggressively carved up cabinets, and ripped clothes were scattered all around me. I had to shuffle my feet to make a path through the debris. I made a quick stop to check out the garage, then I left the property. This house left a lasting impression on me. Witnessing all the vandalism and disregard for the previous family's home left me feeling quite melancholy.

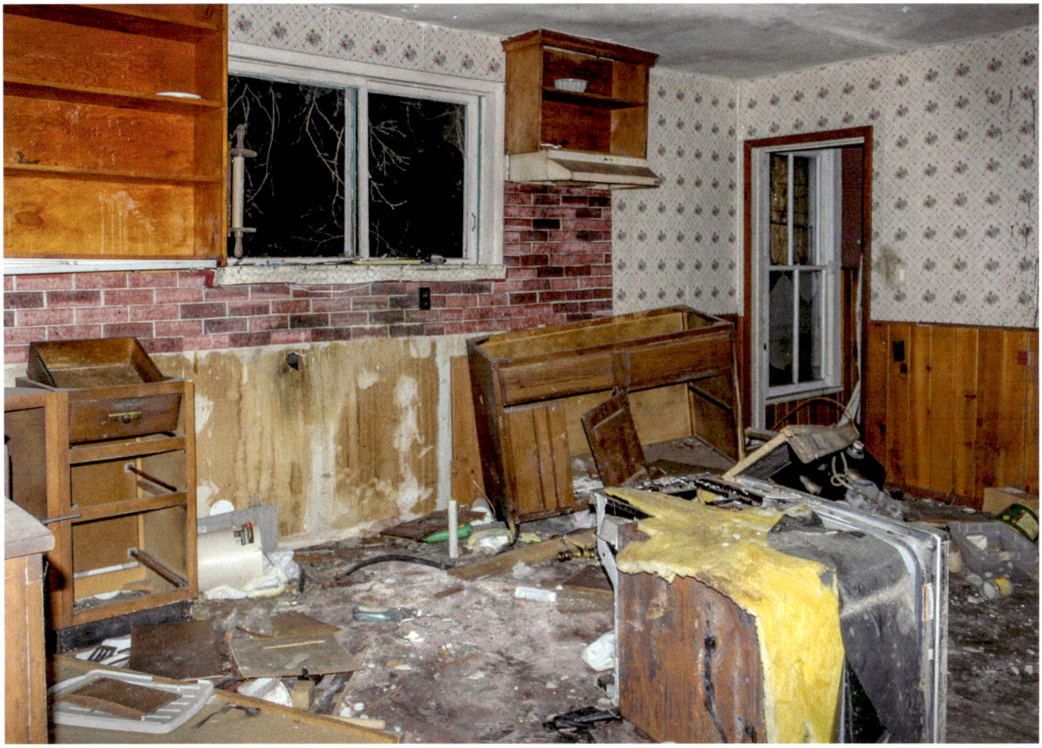

The kitchen lies in a chaotic state of demolition.

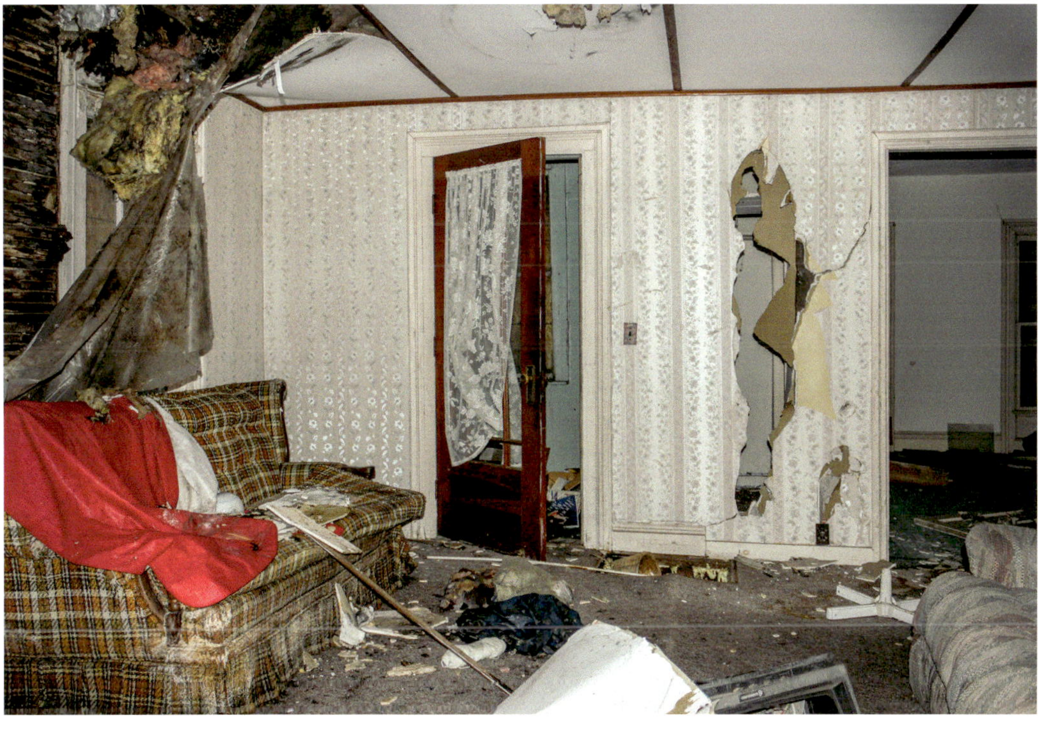

Insulation and debris sit comfortably on the couch of this desecrated living room.

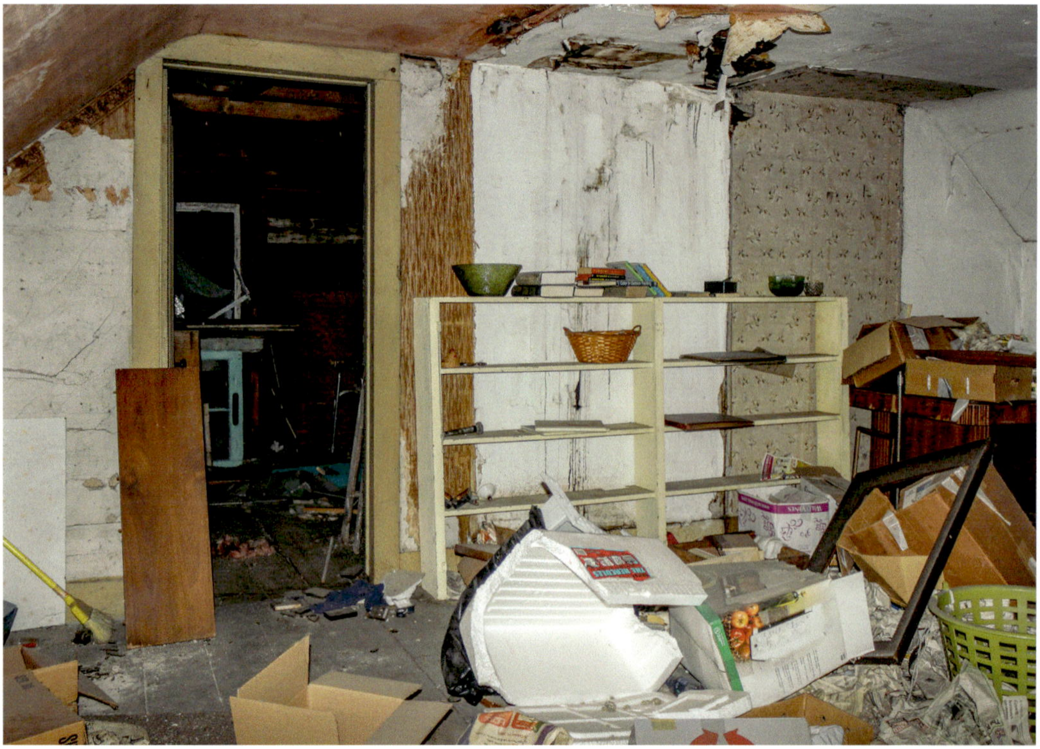

Smashed items litter the floor, leading to an old wood-working room.

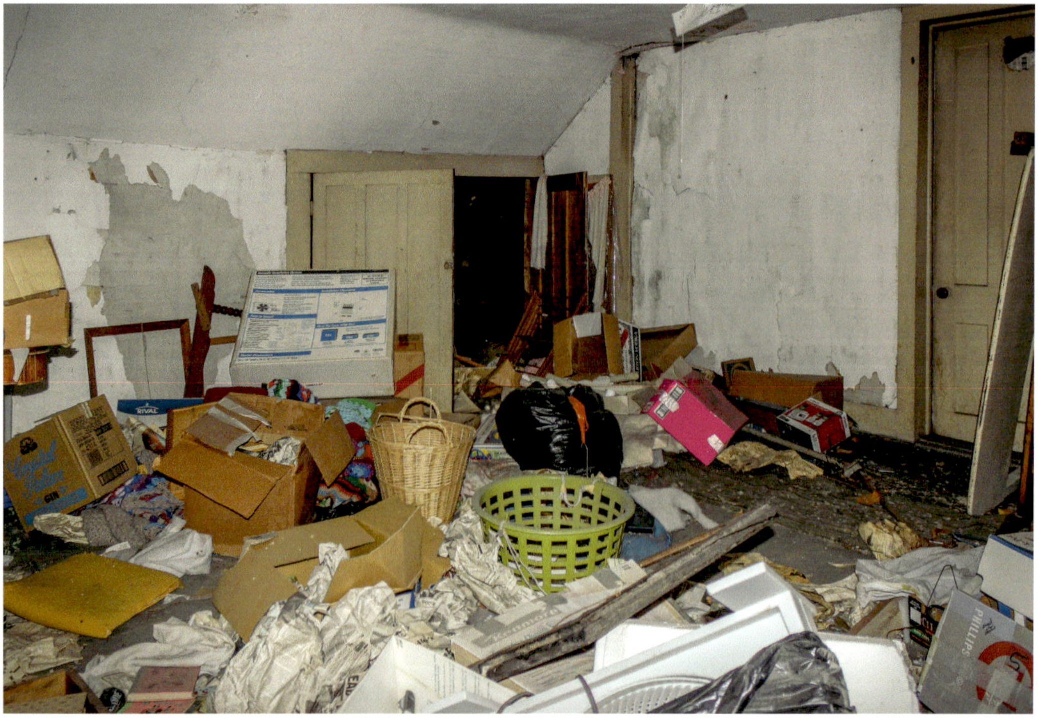

A pan of my camera to my right, reveals a crawlspace that must have piqued the interest of intruders.

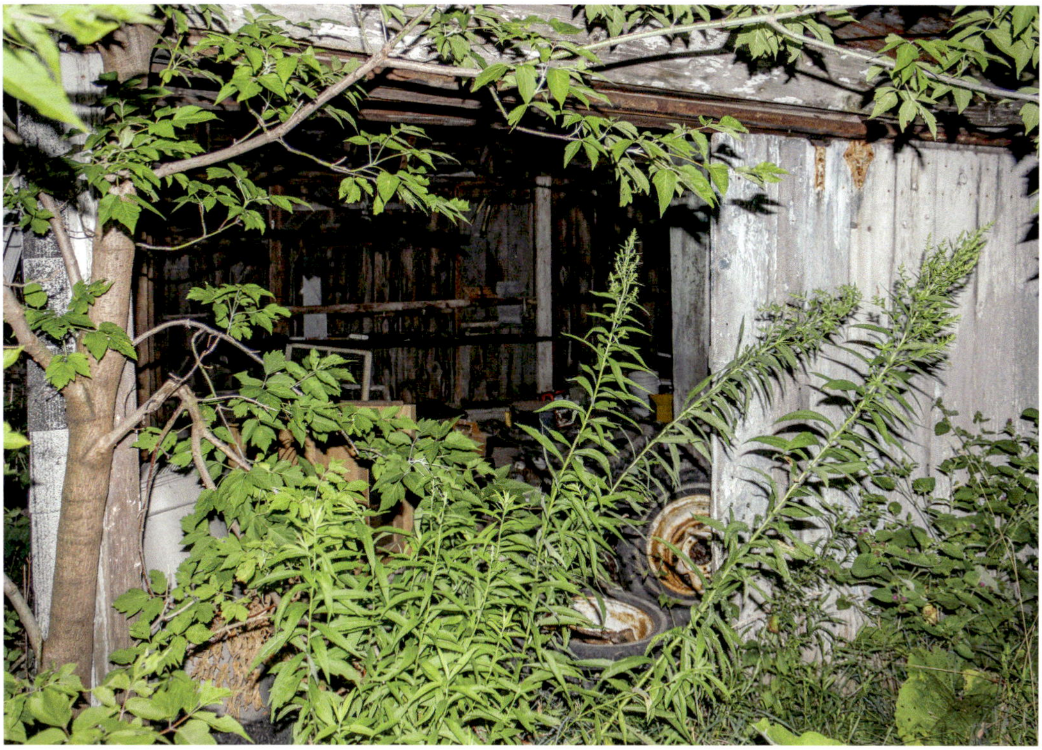

The entrance to the garage, veiled by trees and bushes.

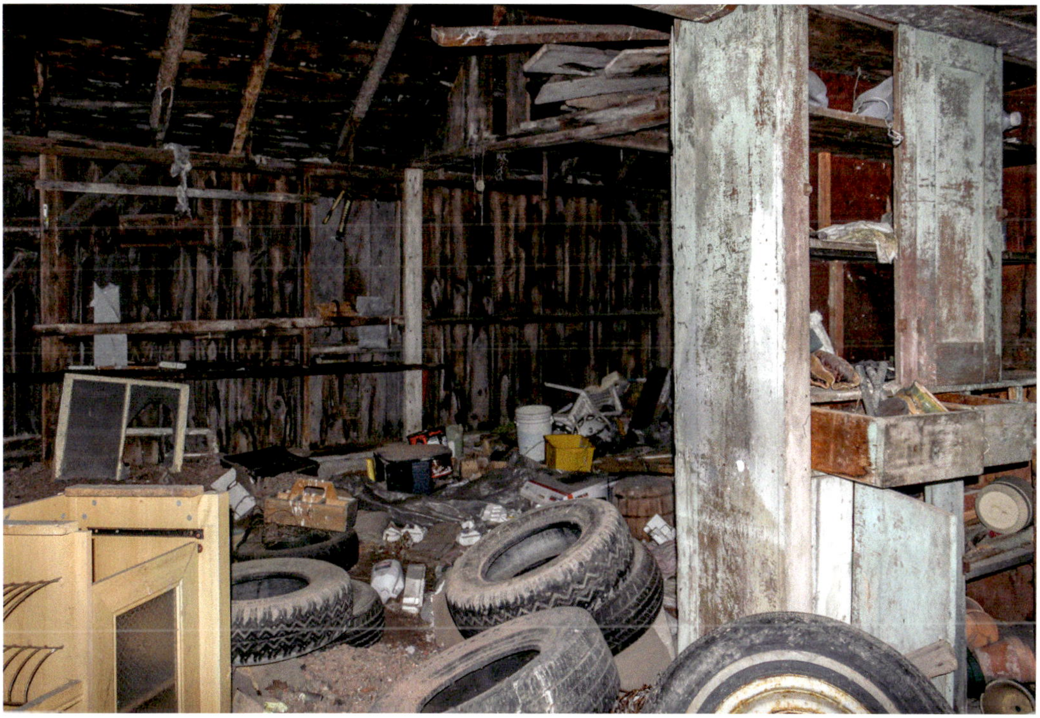

The garage bore the same fate as the interior of the house, with its contents dismantled and strewn about.

12

ST. REGIS PAPER MILL

1899-1985

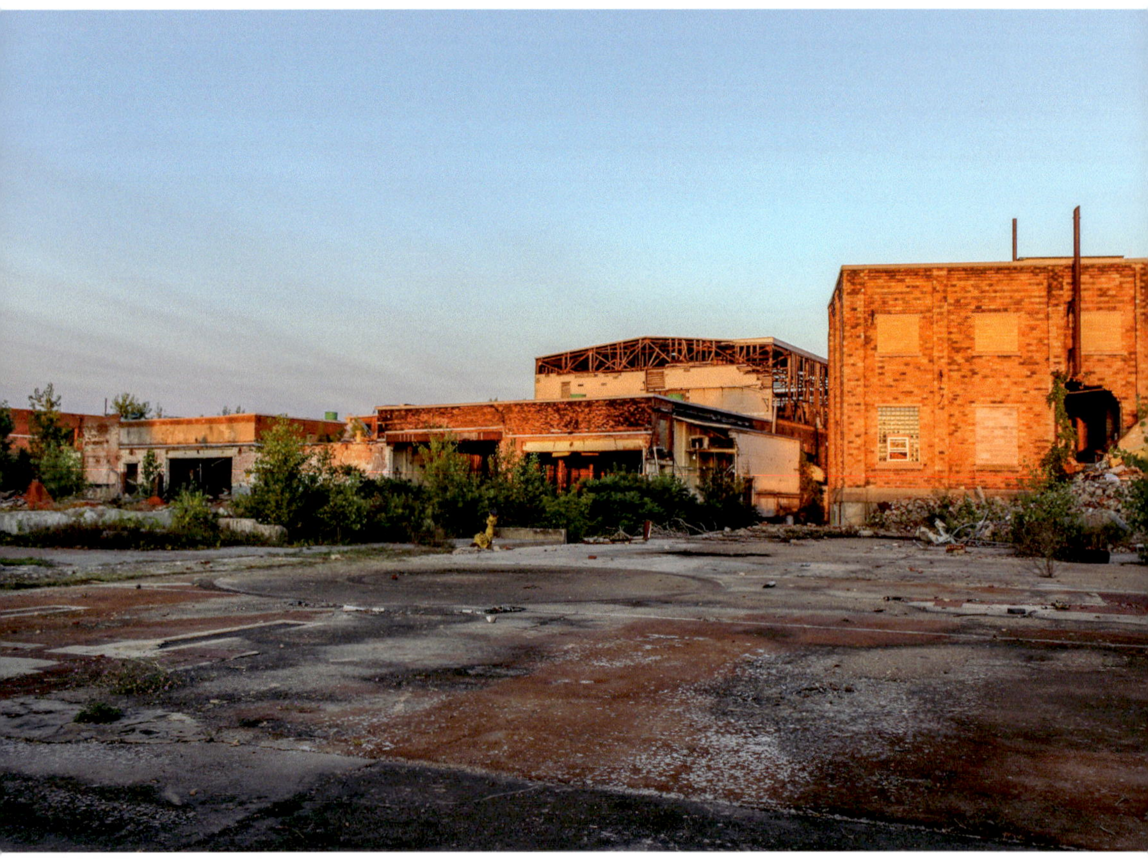

Since its establishment, the St. Regis Paper Mill would grow to become one of the leading newsprint manufacturers in the region. During its peak, in the mid-1950s, this mill employed roughly 900 people. It is said that the surrounding town of Deferiet, NY, was originally created to house to mills multitude of workers.

Of all the abandoned locations I have discovered and documented, the St. Regis Paper Mill holds the number one spot as my favorite exploration. I came to know it first by word of mouth, then by the countless times she lured me back. It was too good to be true; twelve buildings, easy access, and great photo opportunities, what more could an explorer want? Crawling under the barbed-wire fence, I became immediately overwhelmed. I had no idea where to start. With endless photo opportunities, I decided to head into the closest building. I managed to find blueprints of the mill, rolled up in a bin in the first building I entered. This incredible find revealed the exact role each building played as well as their wireframe dimensions. My first shot of the blueprints was what I would use as my guide every time I returned. With night rapidly encroaching, and no lighting at my disposal, I had to leave. I returned the next day, and the following day, as well as many other days after that. This location had so much to offer—the history of the paper mill as well as many photo opportunities. With the discovery into each building, I was sent back in time to experience the mill's working environment during operation. The St. Regis Paper Mill, to this day, is my first "holy grail" of locations explored.

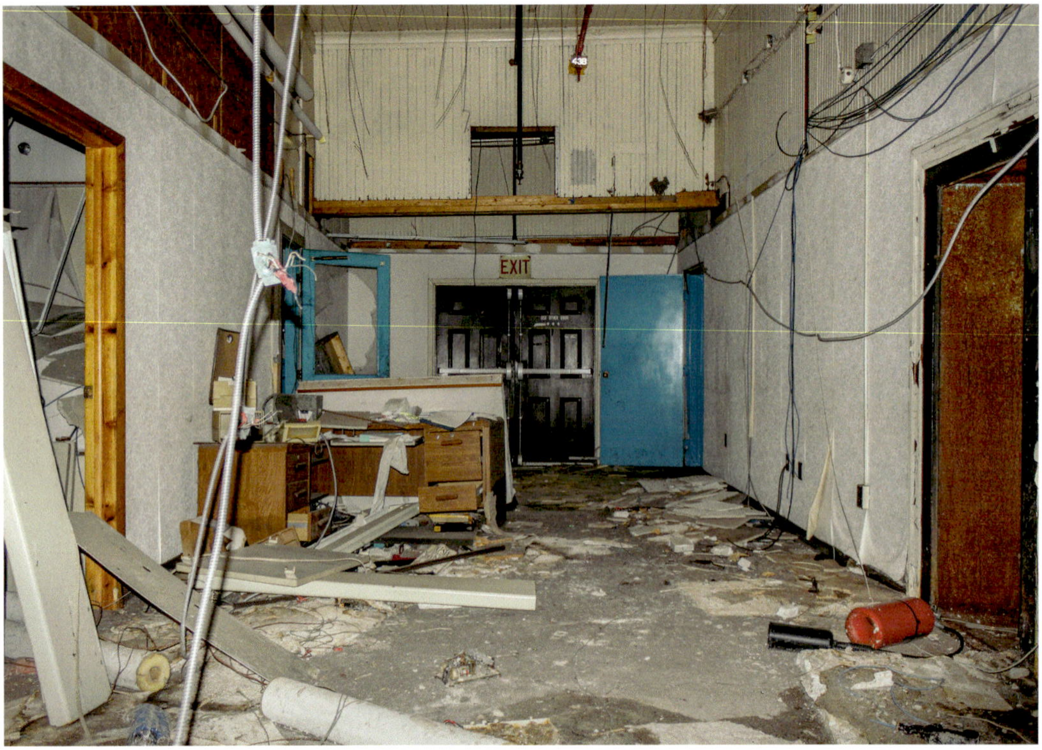

Nakedly exposed and ransacked, a corridor in the administration building.

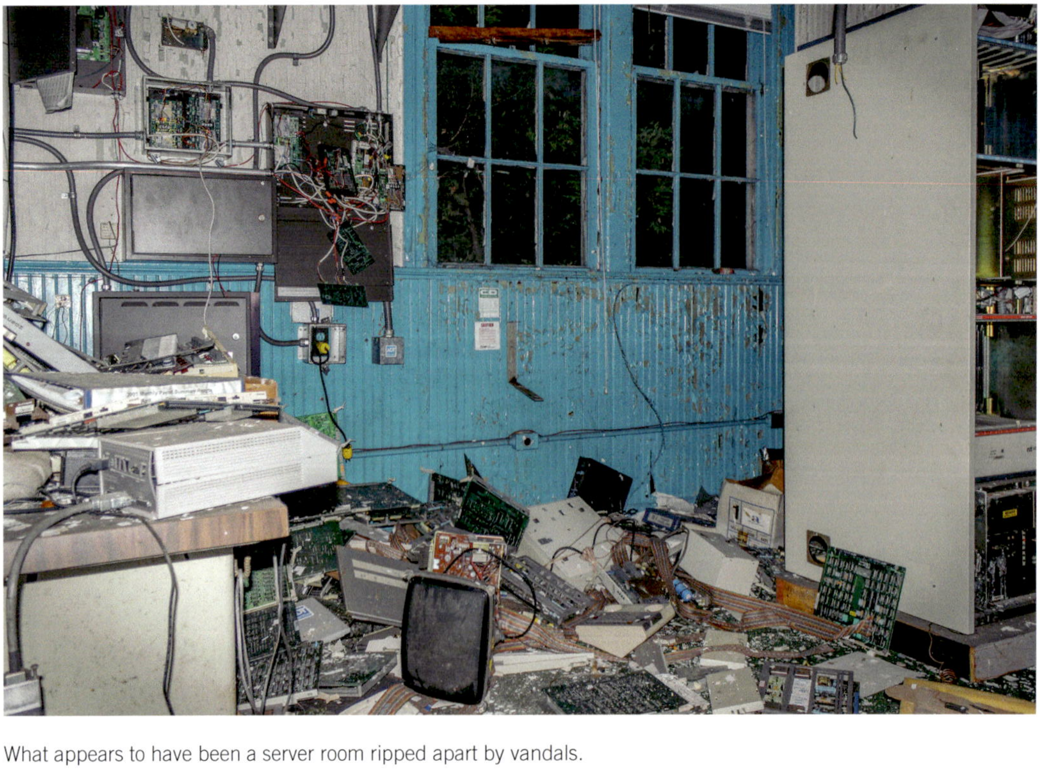

What appears to have been a server room ripped apart by vandals.

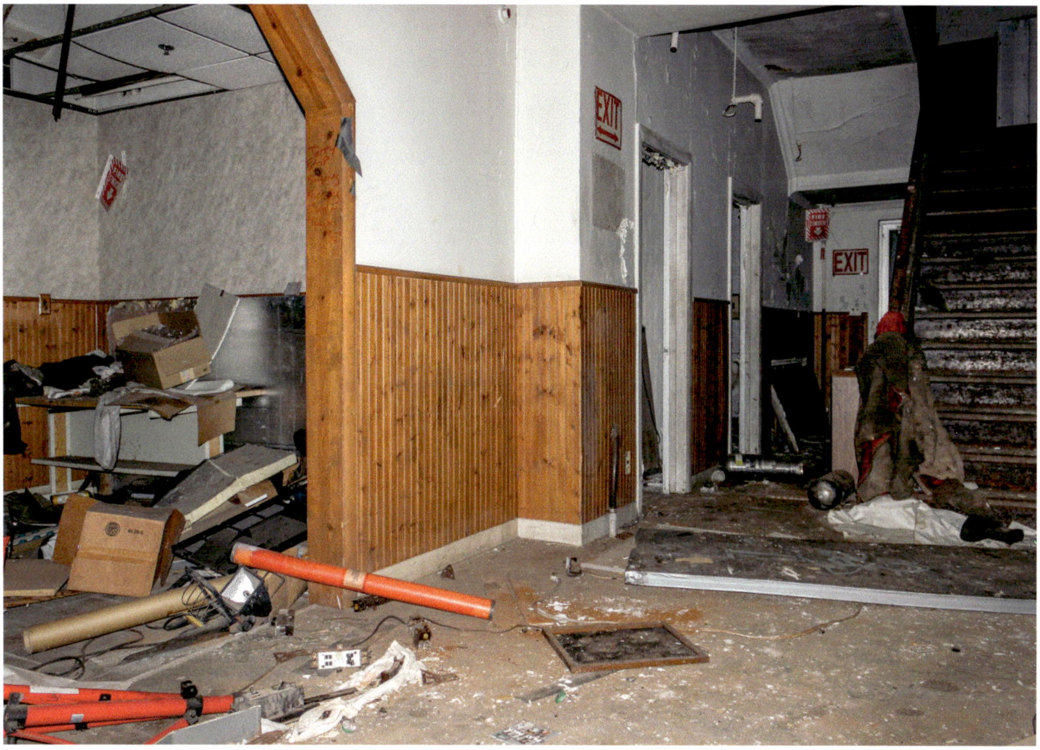

A room crammed full of equipment on the left, with a staircase leading to the second floor on the right.

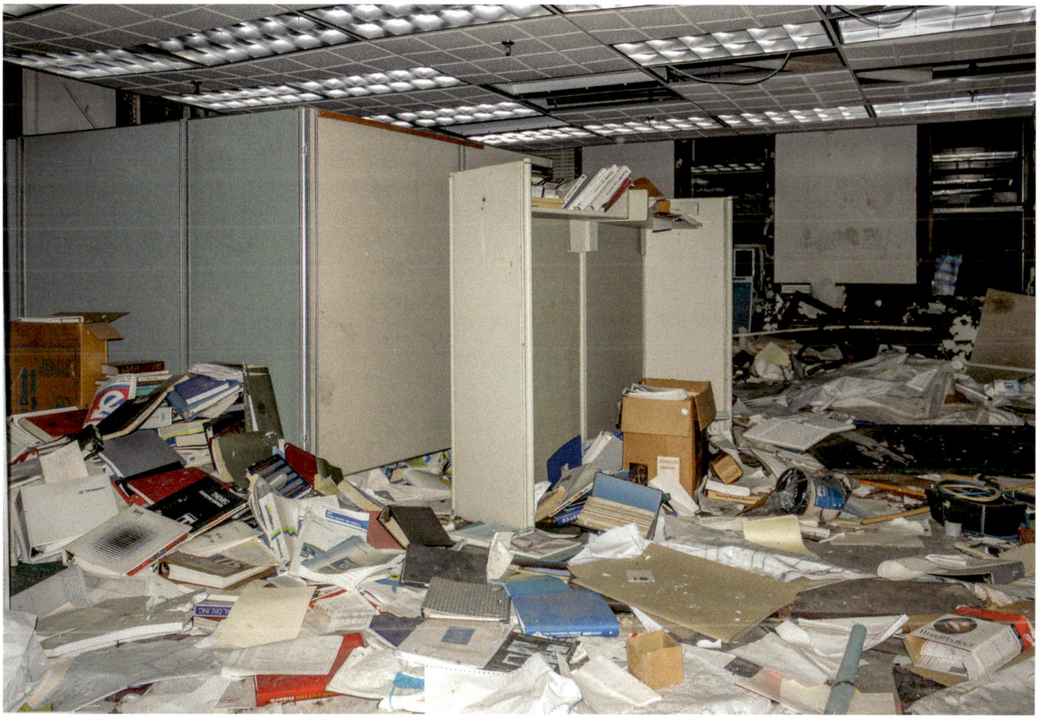

A second-floor office with cubicles, business documents, and binders.

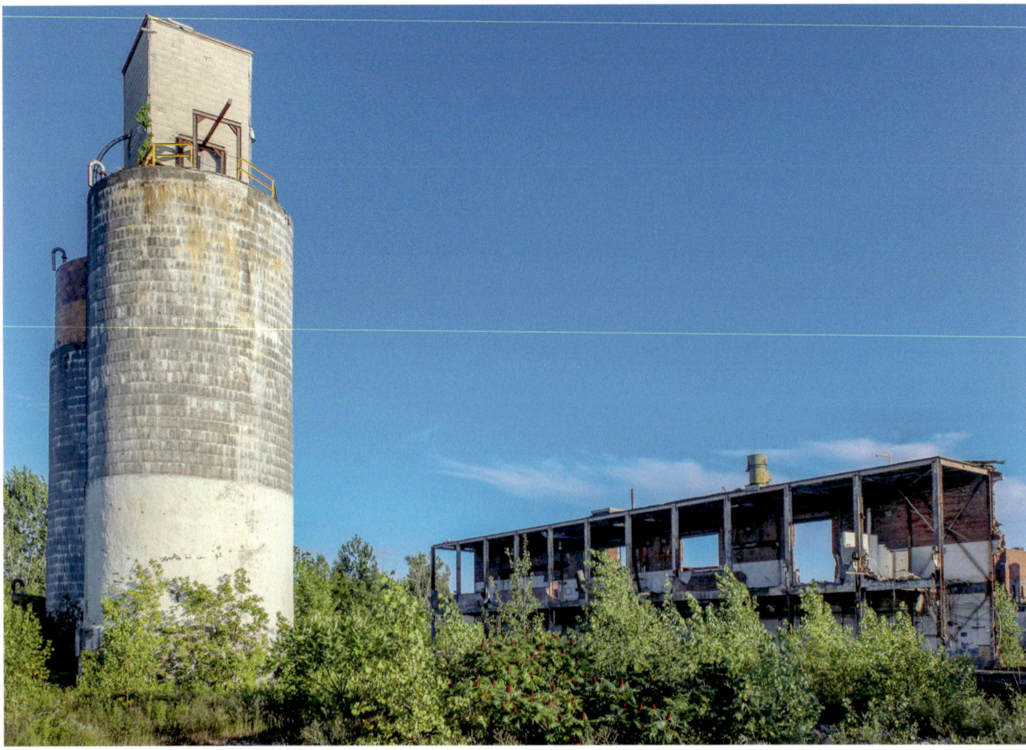

A silo towers over the back entrance to the primary manufacturing section.

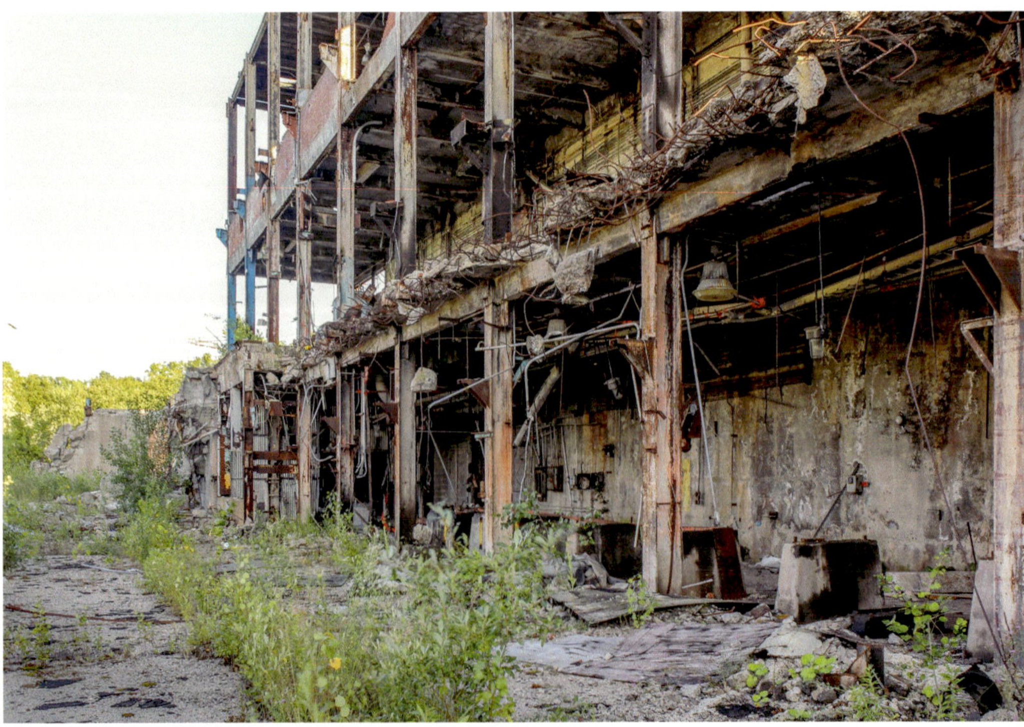

The bare skeleton of this façade; rebar and support beams are all that remain of this small entrance.

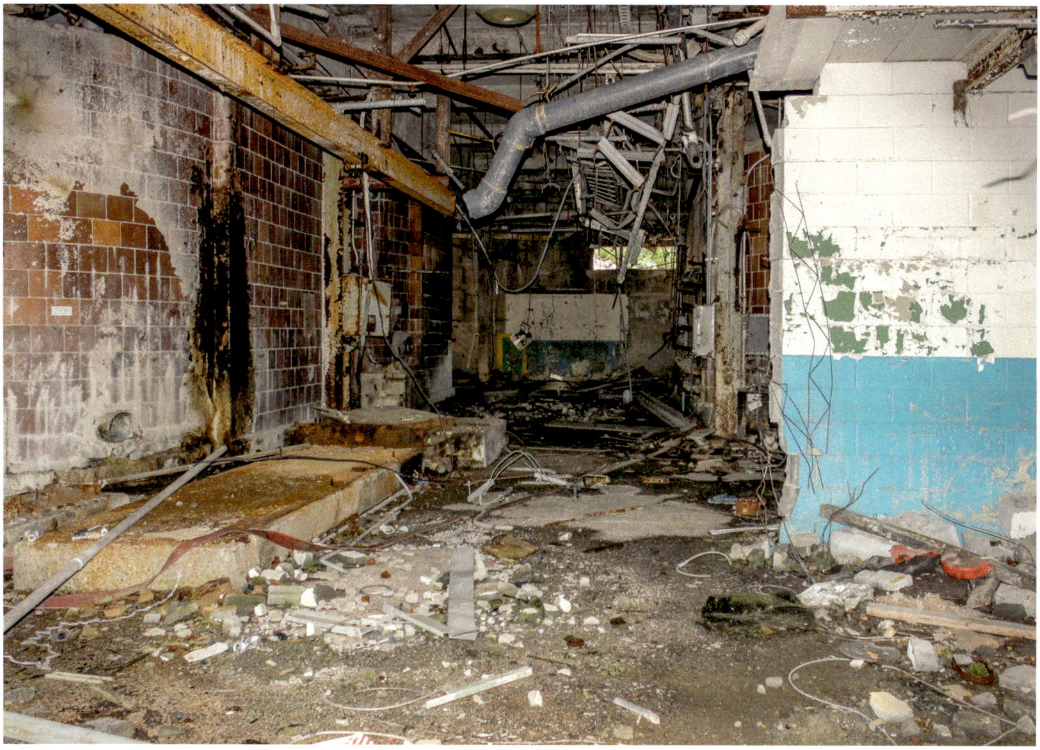

A hallway littered with large brick. Other chambers sit to the left.

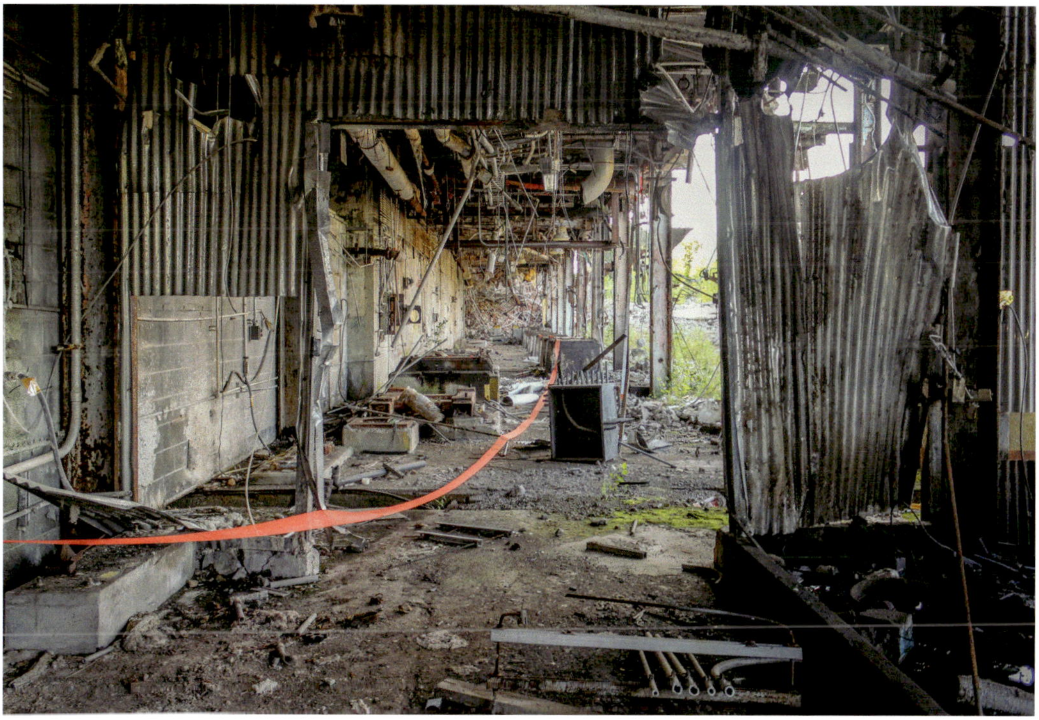

A return glance back through the contorted metal and wires that made up this opening.

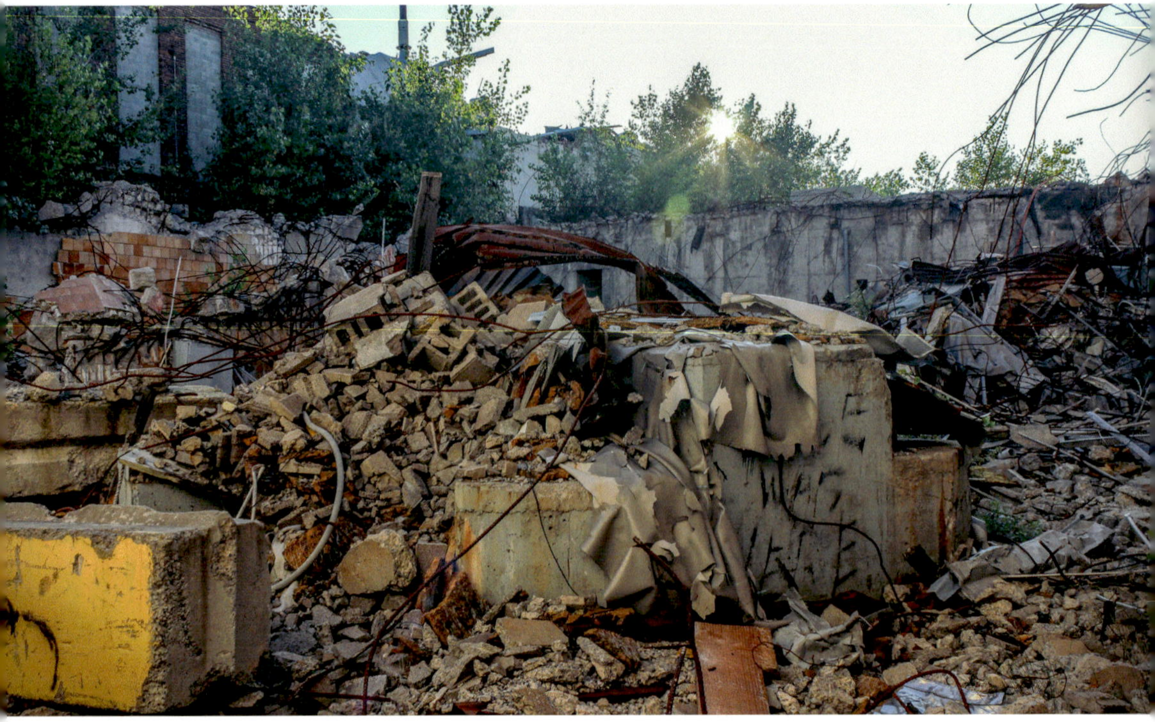

When the company relocated, the machines and equipment were so massive, some walls and foundations had to be destroyed in order to extract them.

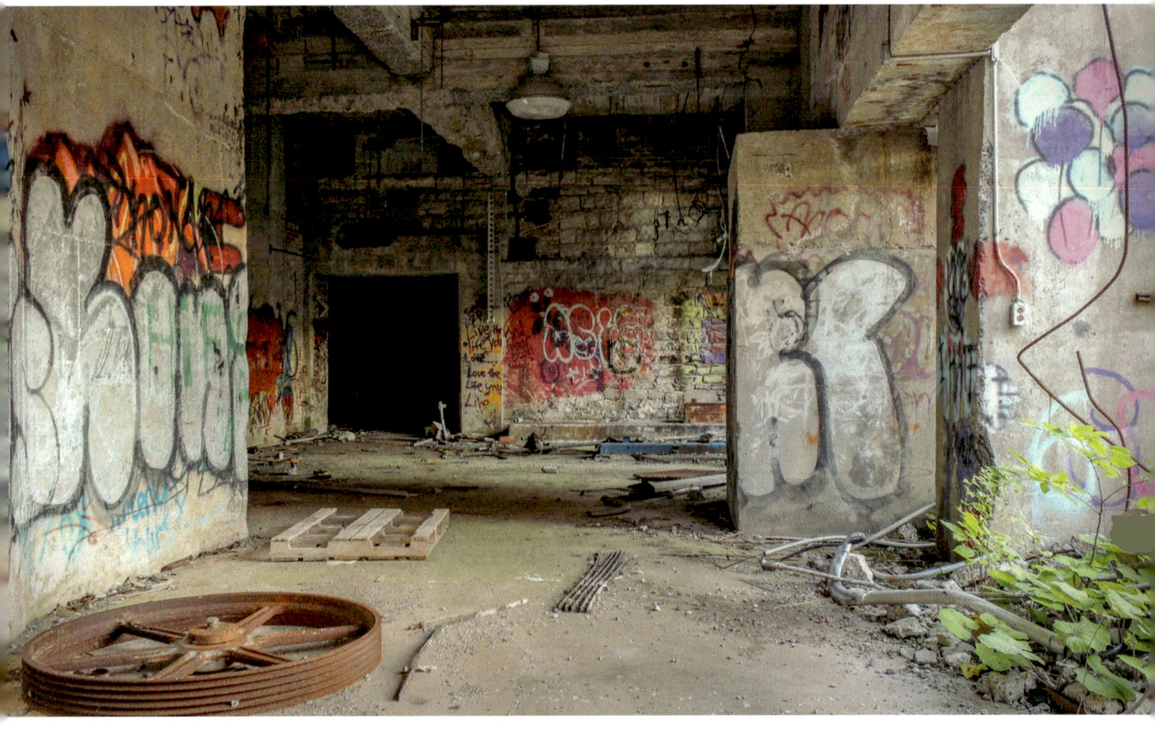

Colorful graffiti welcomes explorers before they enter complete darkness.

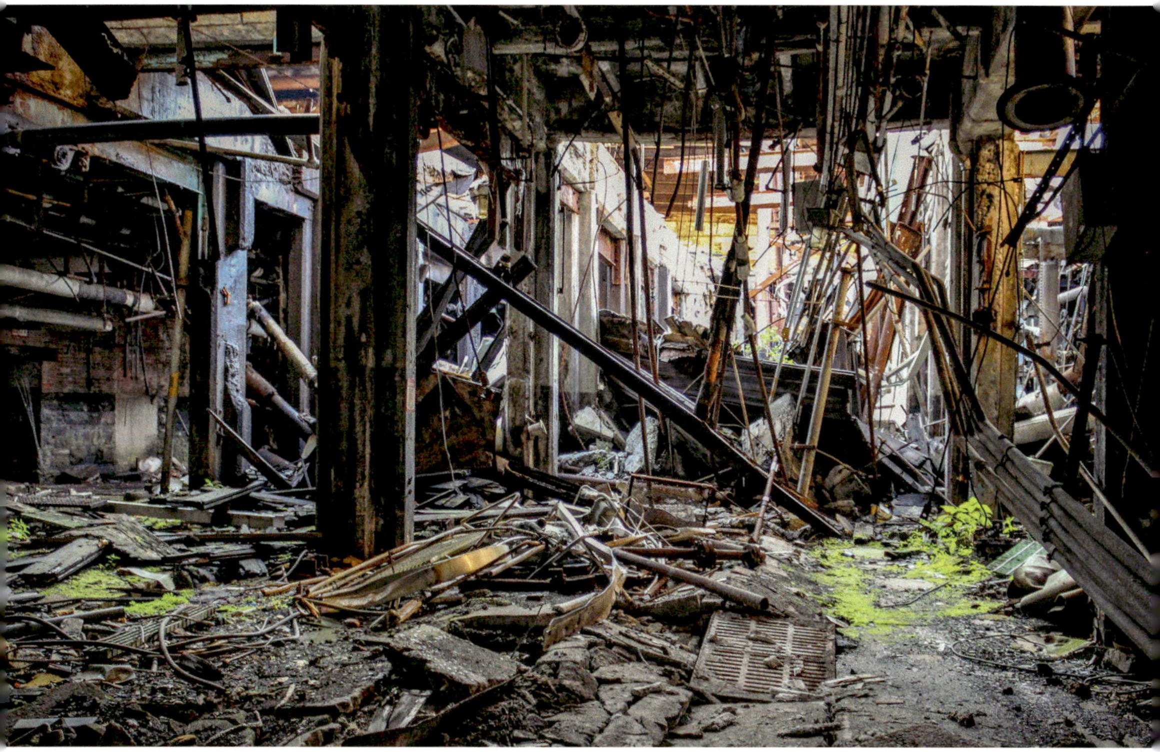

From the first floor, a perspective of a section of collapsed roof.

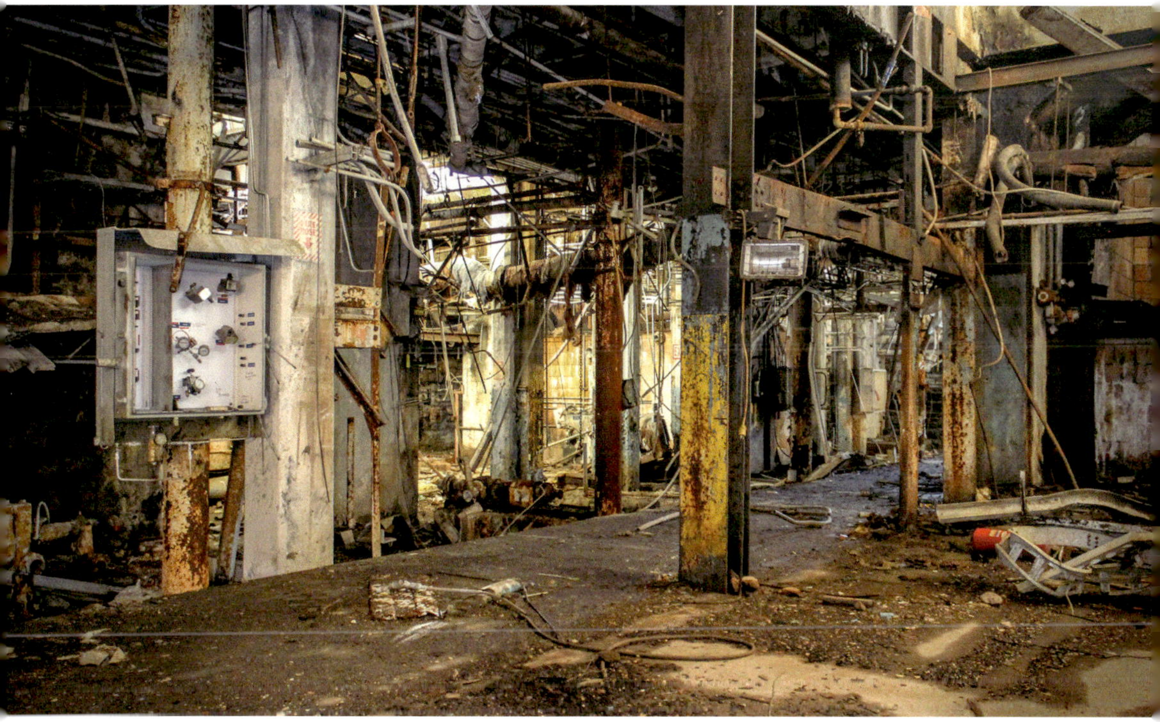

An accessory room to the previous, comprised of hanging pipes and twisted metal.

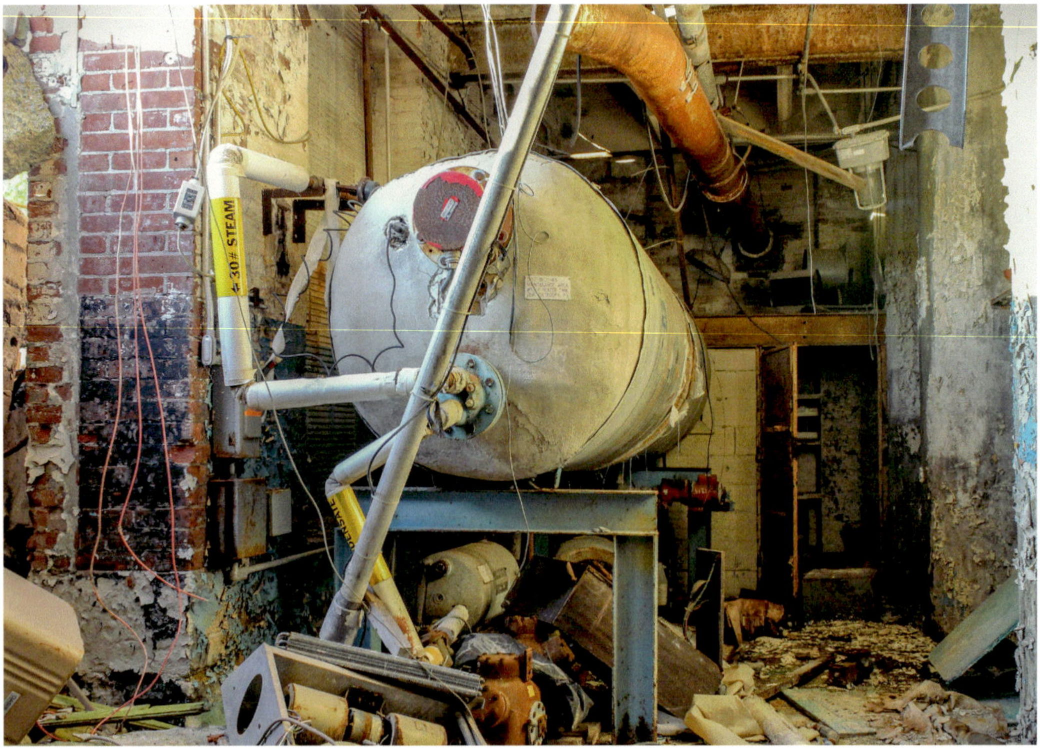

Further in, a large pressure chamber sits sealed in a protective layer of insulation.

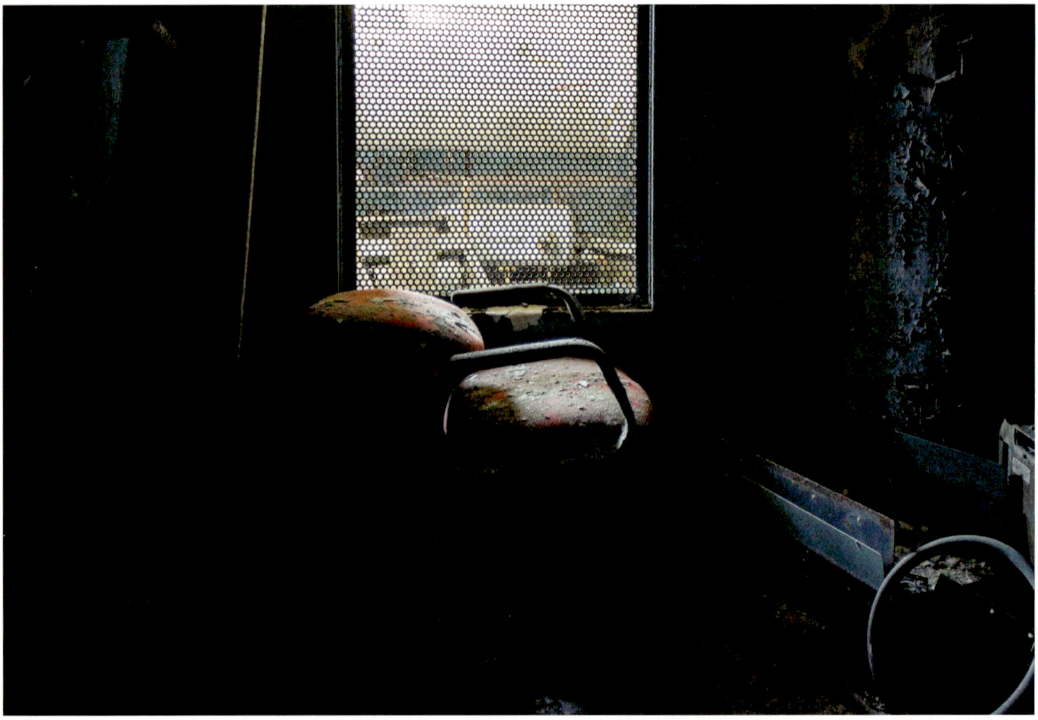

Light falls gracefully onto a dying office chair, in the side room, to the right.

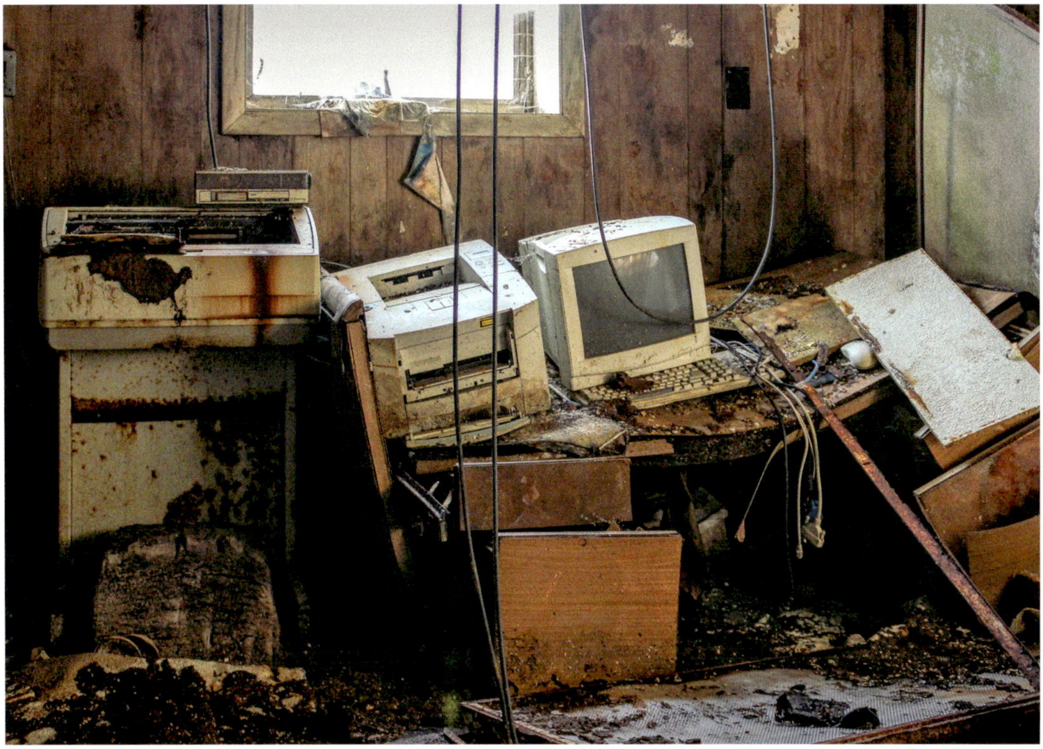

An old desk collapsed under the weight of a desktop and printer.

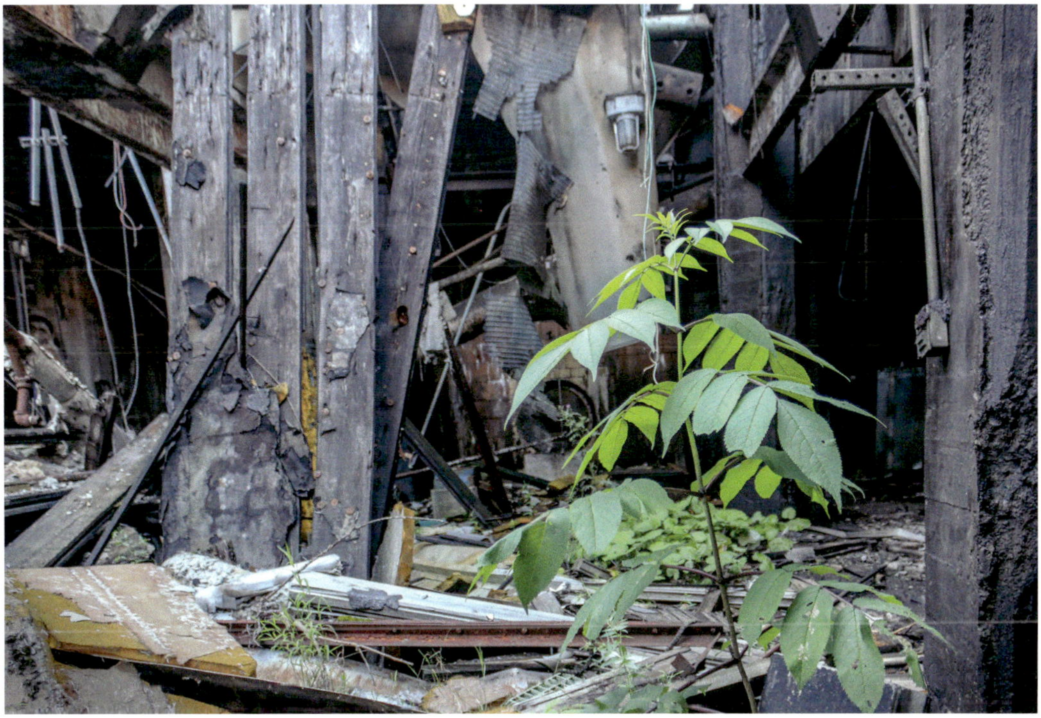

As one life comes to an end, a new life begins.

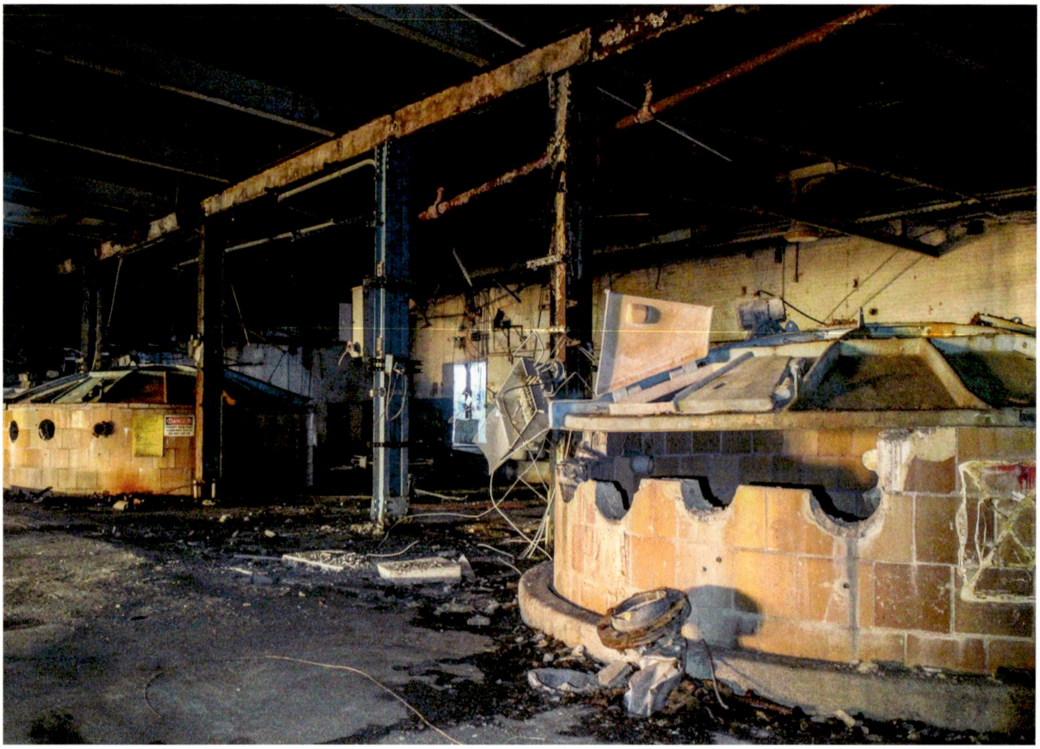

The second floor, a glimpse at the large brick chambers from the top.

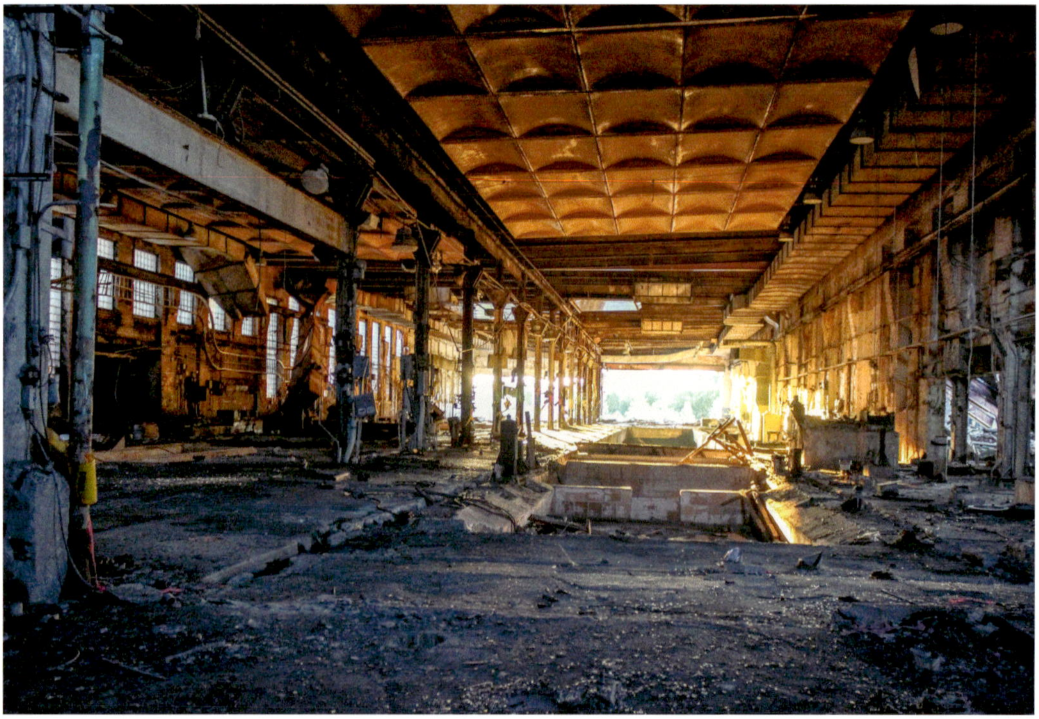

Sunlight wakens this now quiet section of the factory.

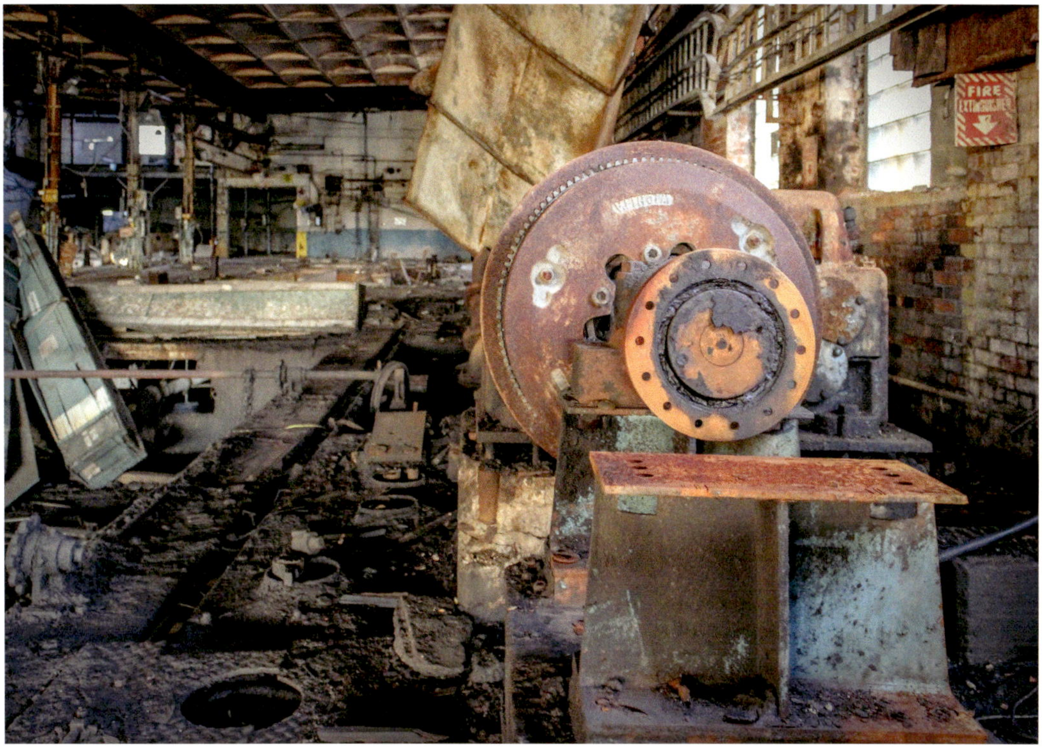

A large machine, its purpose still baffles me.

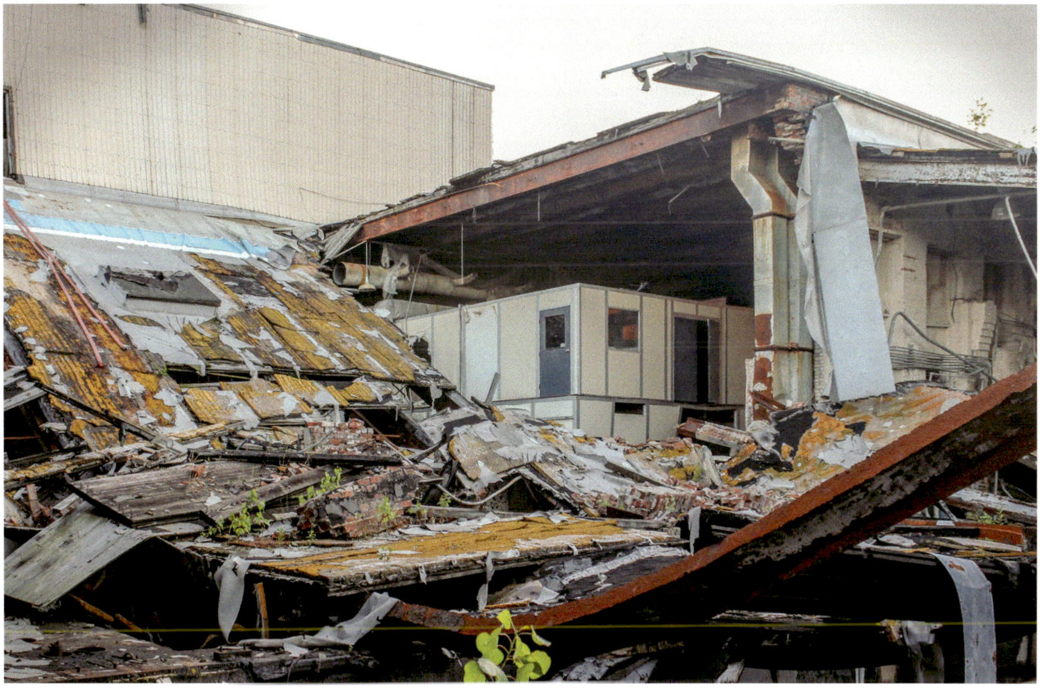

A second floor perspective of the collapsed roof; many years of corrosion have led to the support beams buckling under the weight of the roof.

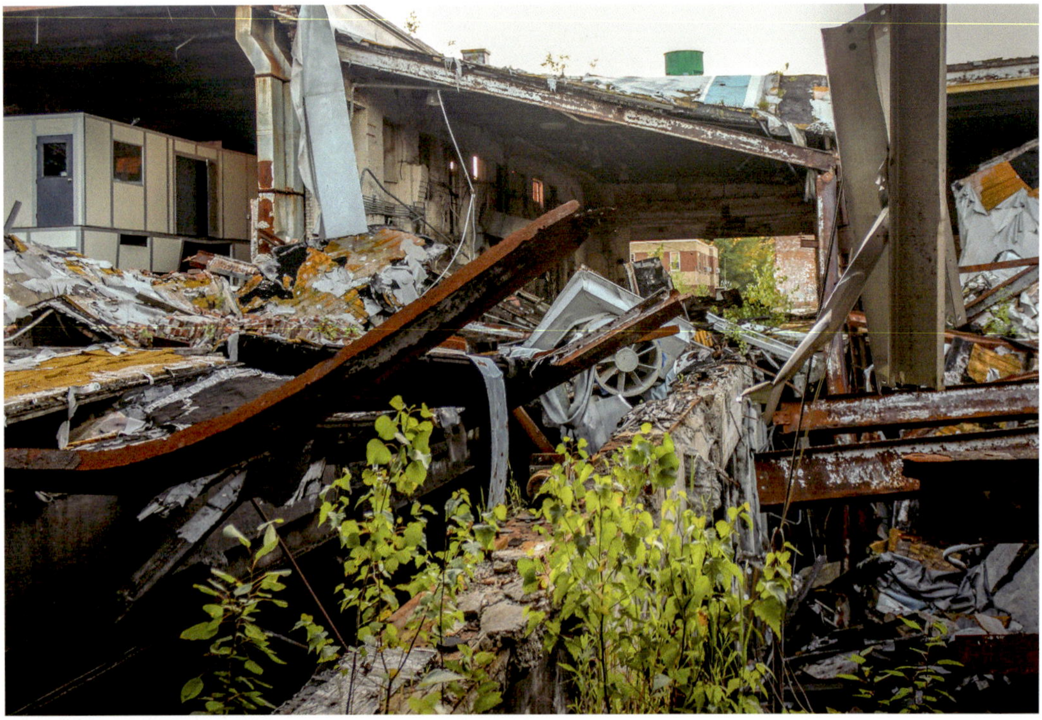

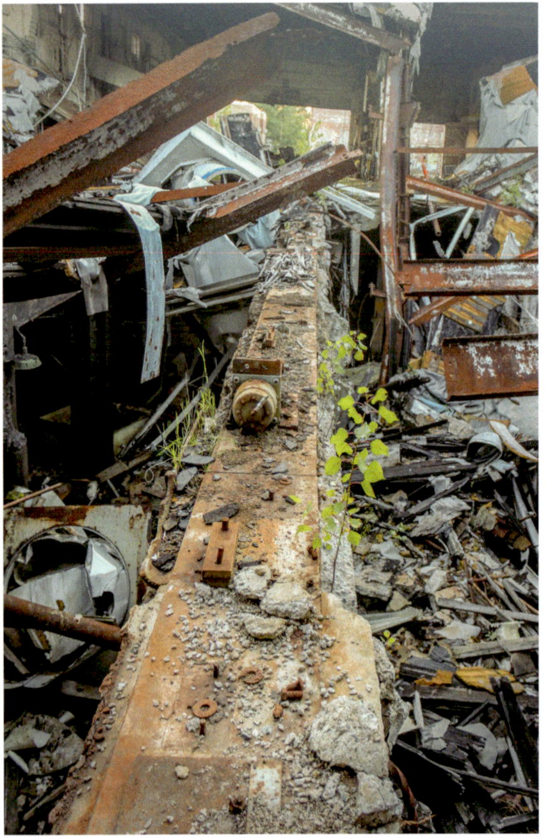

Above: Another glimpse allows the viewer to observe the amount of weight that collapsed the roof.

Left: A central floor joist survived, creating a surface for some plants to miraculously take root in the concrete crumbles.

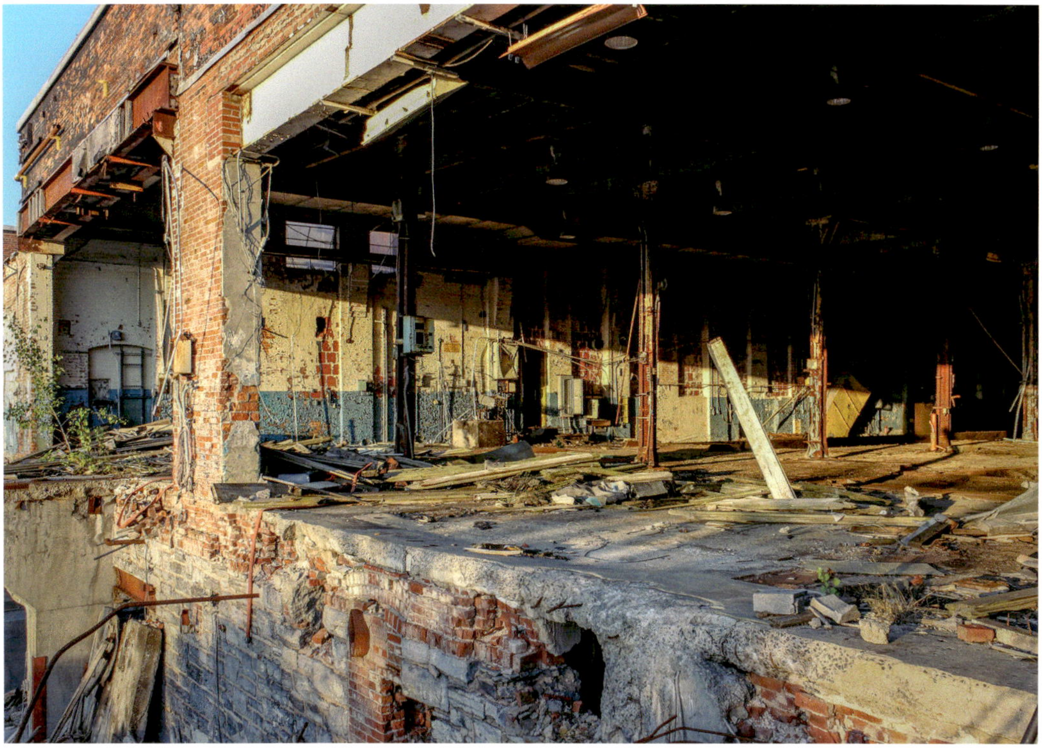

A section where a neighboring roof collapsed.

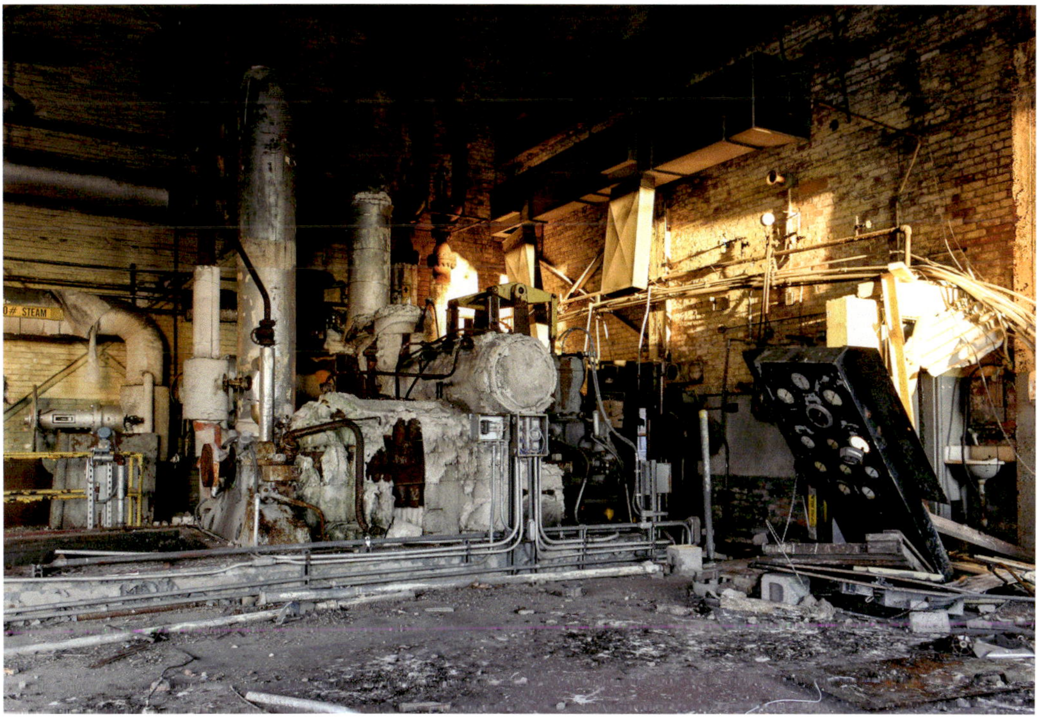

A room on the third level, which appeared to be a steam management system.

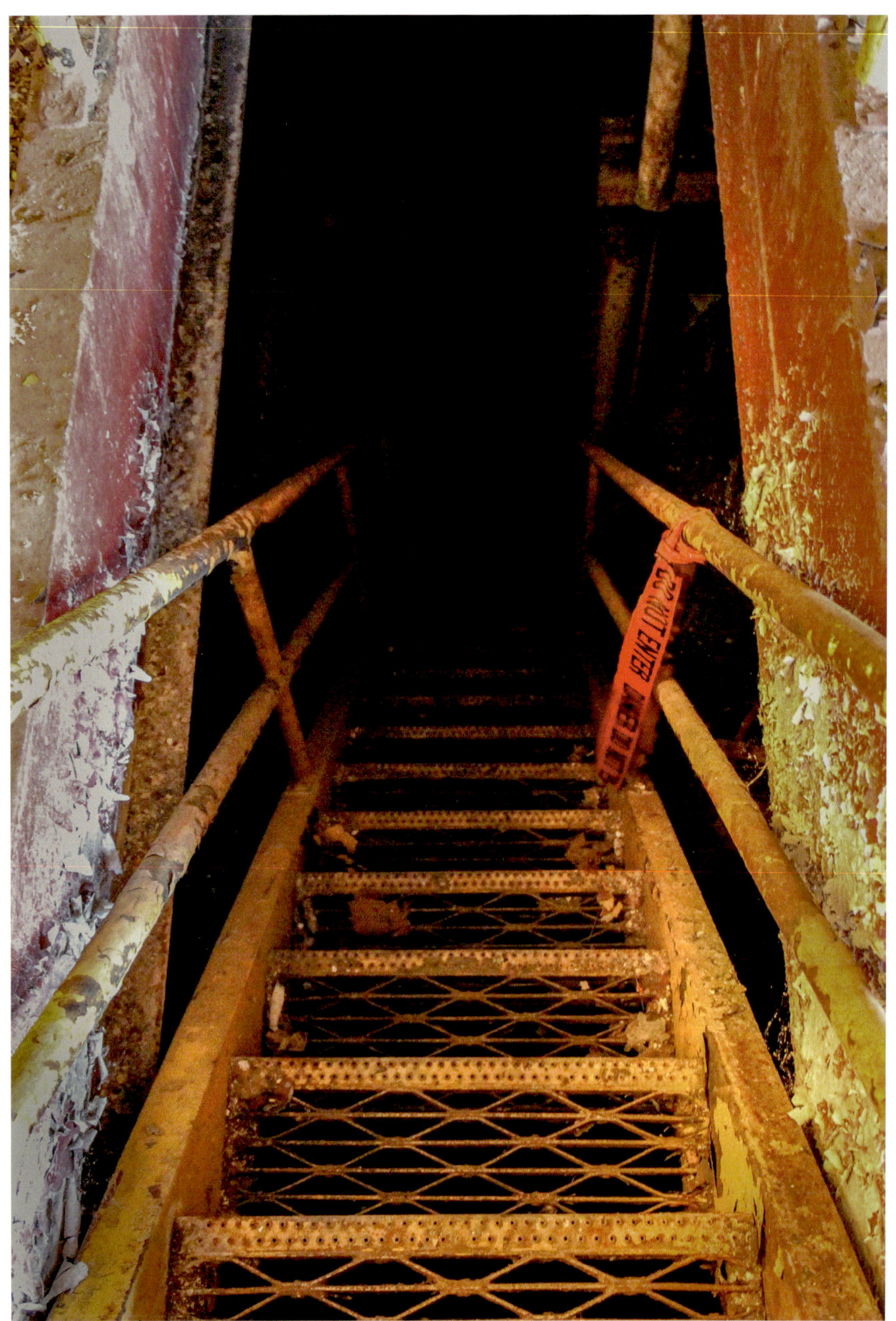

A look down the stairs which lead to a third-level room.

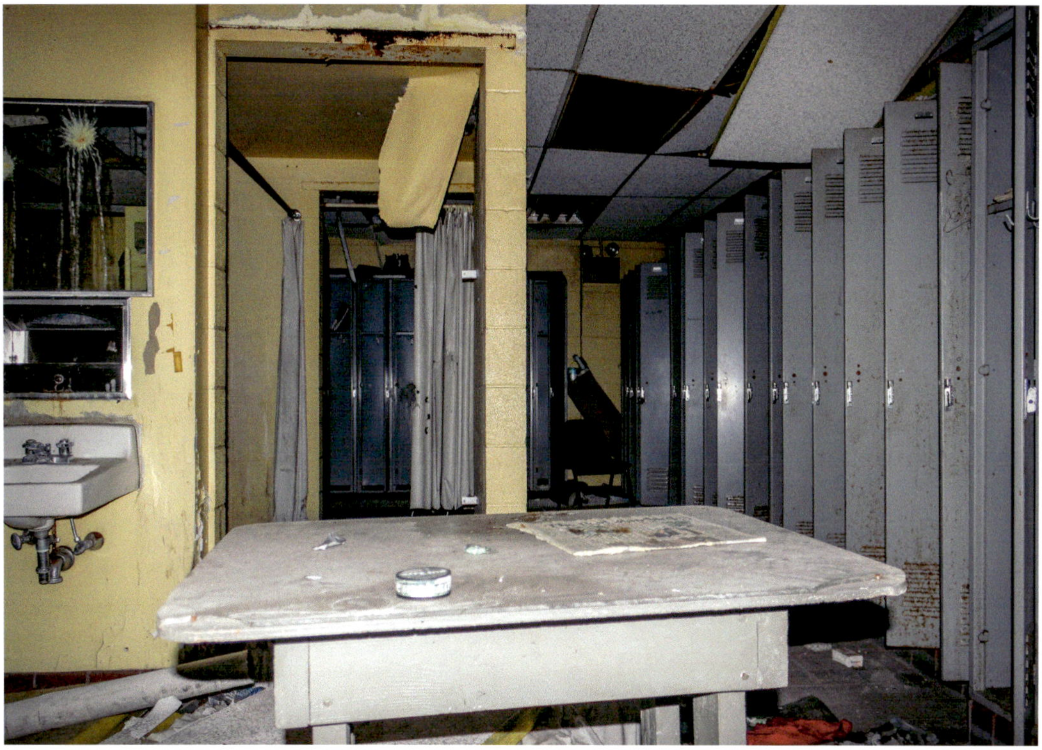

One of many locker rooms, on the first floor, of the primary manufacturing building.

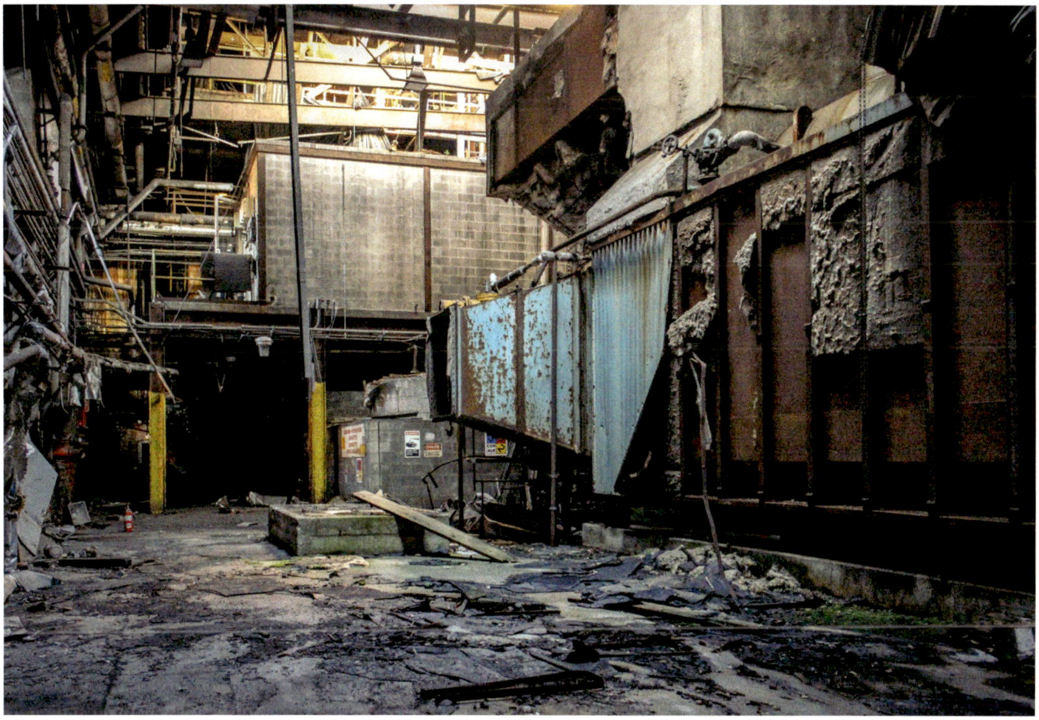

Entrance to the chemical section of the mill.

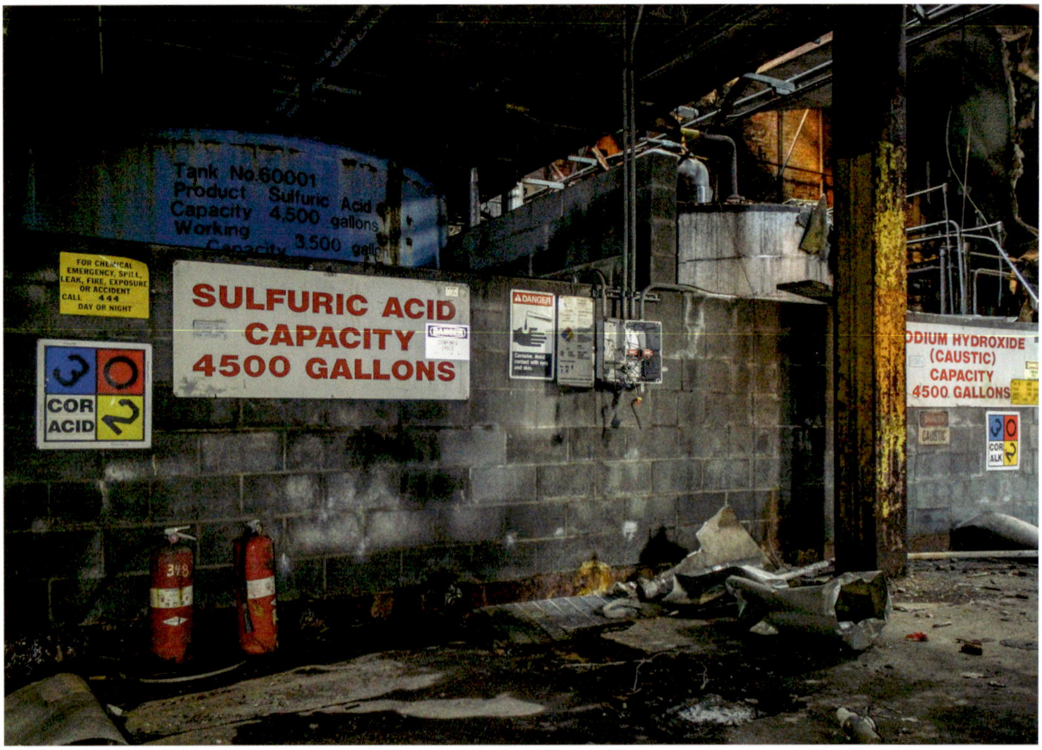

Massive vats still containing chemicals, left-over by the company.

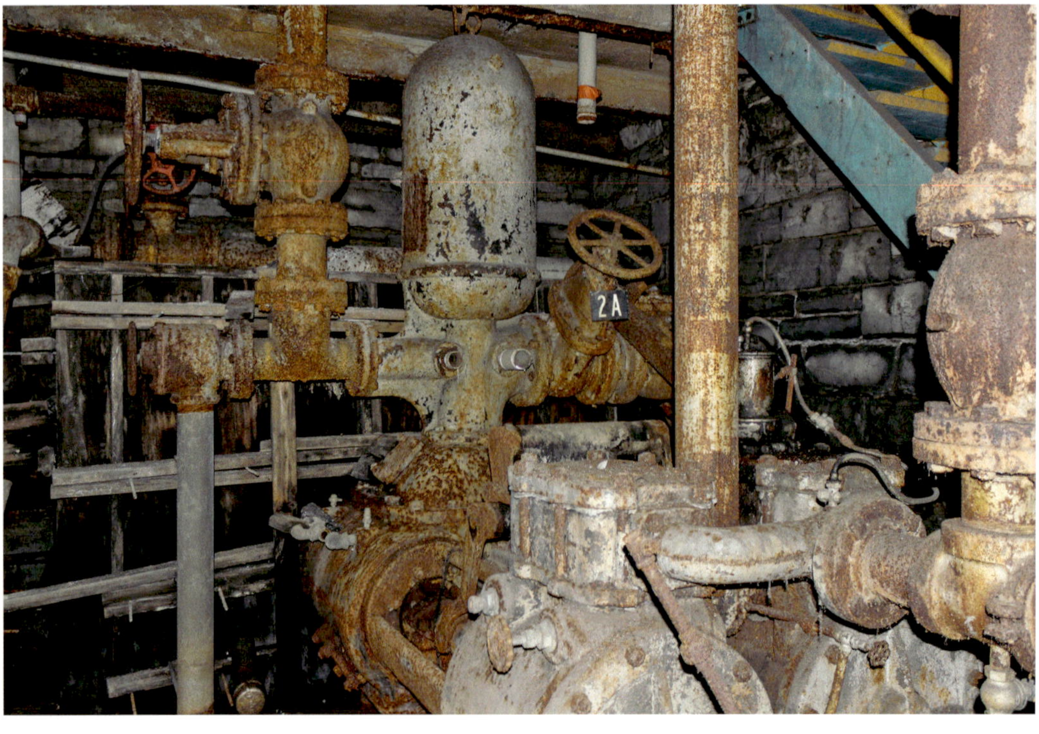

A conjunction of rusty pipes lie under a staircase at the end of the building.

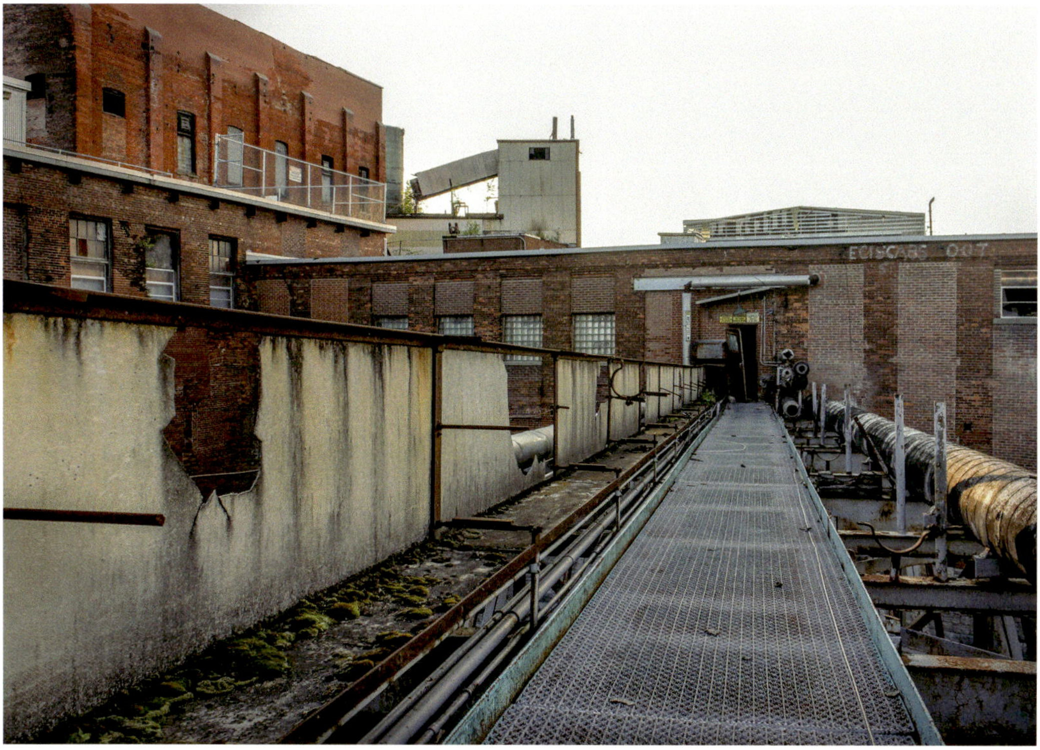

A photo from the bridge, overlooking a river that used to power the mill.

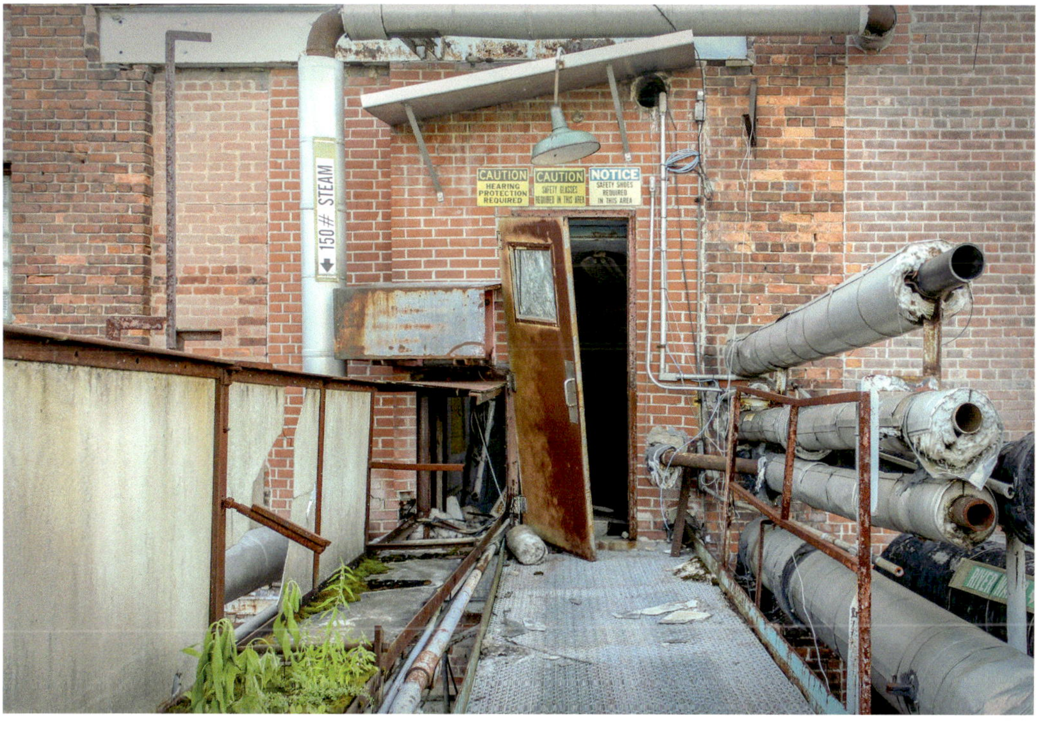

A closer look at an intruder's desperate attempt to access the bridge.

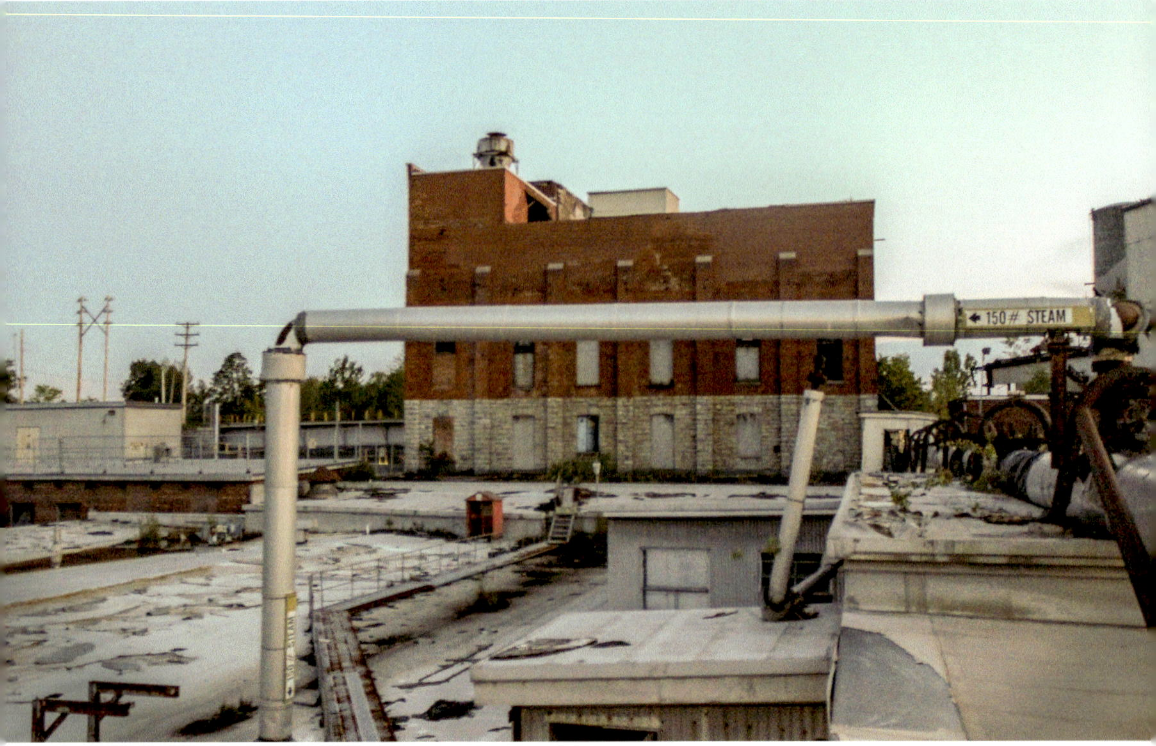

An opening to this roof led me to a very dangerous section of the mill.

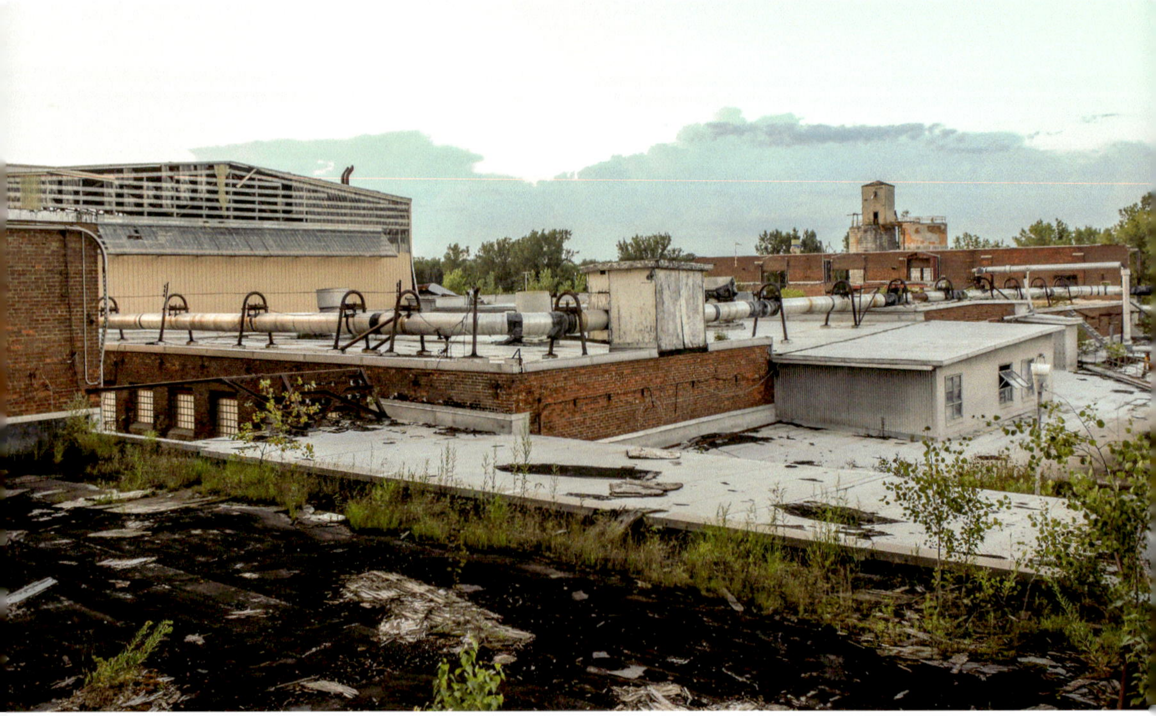

Looking back after a long walk across this menacing catwalk led me to a very unstable section of the mill.

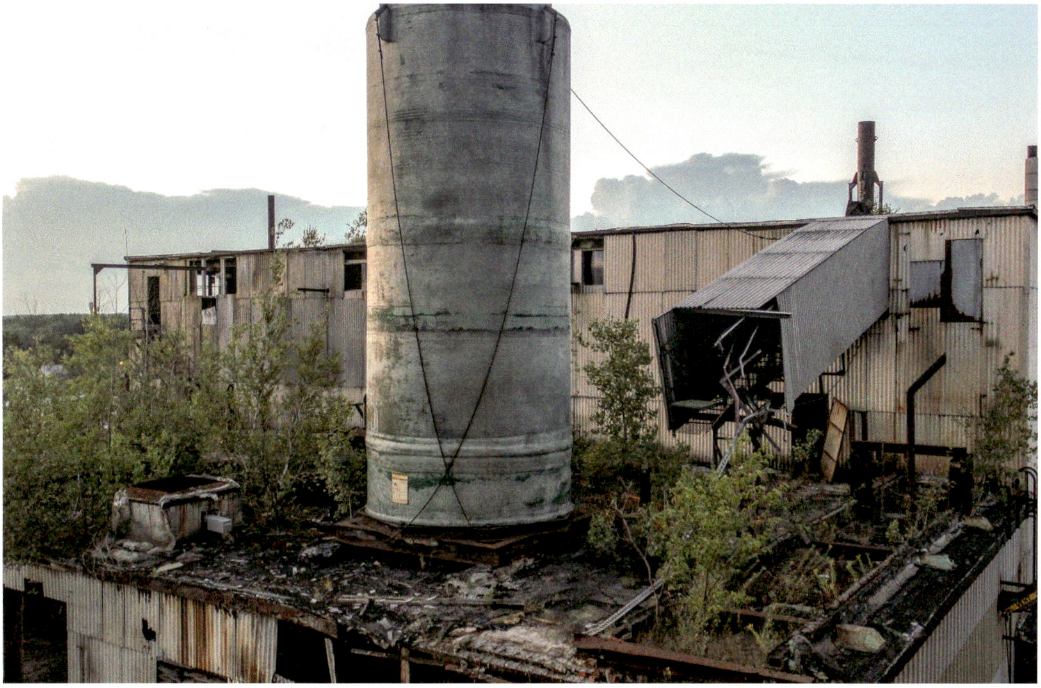

With only a sheet of plywood holding me forty feet above twisted metal and concrete, this was one of the scariest shots I took on this exploration.

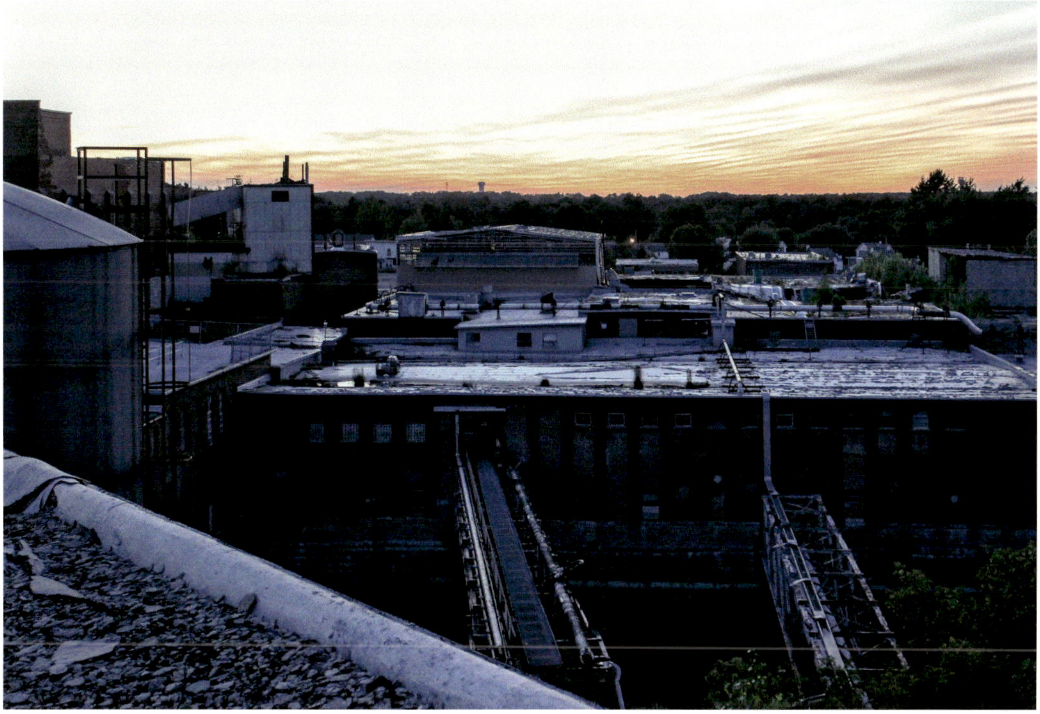

I found a path that led to a few remaining buildings across the river. I climbed up to the roof, collected my thoughts, and enjoyed this beautiful sunset over the St. Regis Paper Mill.

13

TJ'S REPAIR SHOP

Active Dates Unknown

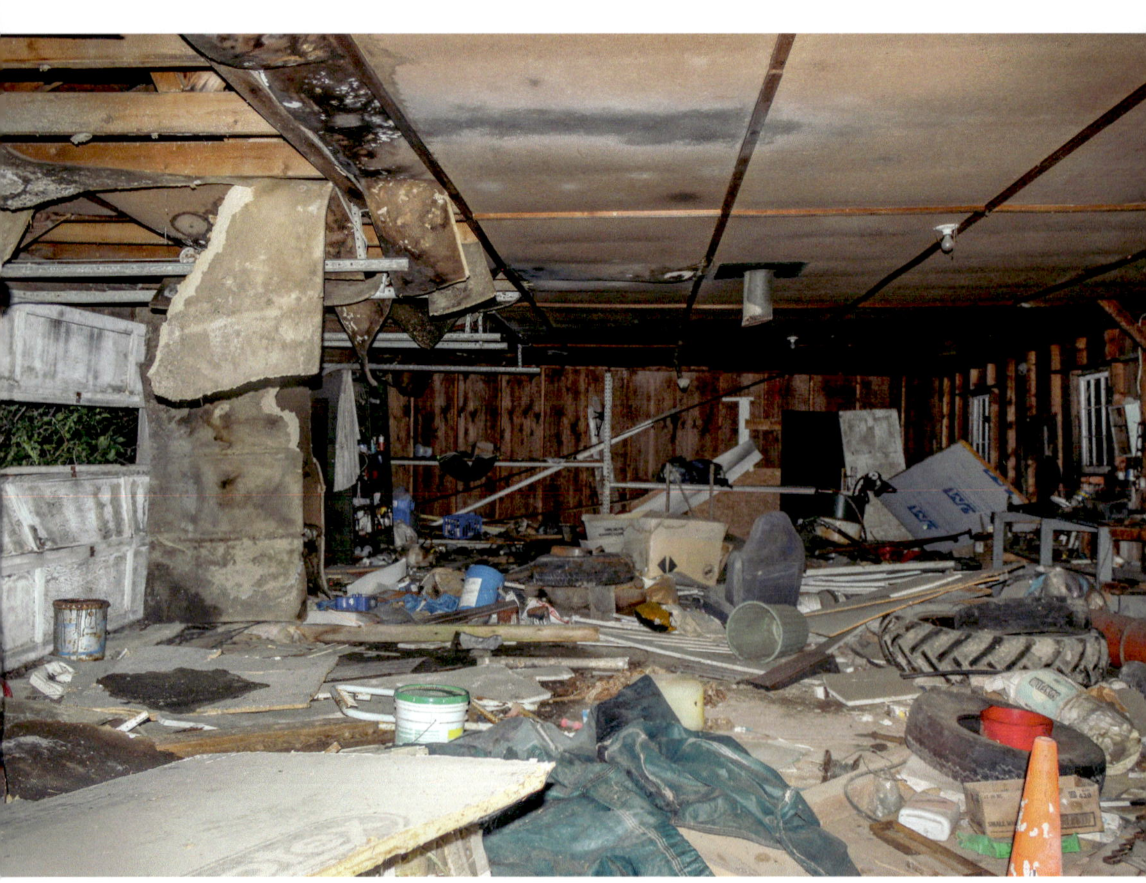

I first discovered this formation of buildings while I was driving to the Abbass Food Corporation. I decided to check them out on the way back. A few hours passed and I returned to the plot of land to investigate. The grass soared above me, in some parts providing the perfect camouflage, as I made my way to the closest building, a barn. Barns are notably messy, so walking through and seeing the assortment of animal bones and skulls was no surprise. I offhandedly flipped on a light switch and with immediate panic, the whole barn lit up. The barn still had power, creating a vast glowing distraction for drivers passing by. I quickly flipped off the switch and the adrenaline slowly left my body. I left the barn and headed over to the second building. This was a house, and as I walked in, I hastily threw on my respirator as I noticed black mold everywhere. Evidence of severe water damage made my choices to step very scarce. Water-logged wood warped under my feet as I made my way to the second floor, only to find an increase in mold and water damage. Fearing that I might fall through the floor, I decided it was time to leave this house. The garage was the last building to explore, and its door had a section that had been pried open on the bottom right side. Lucky for me, it was large enough to fit through. I walked around debris and discarded items searching for any evidence of this place's past life. Then I found it! An old billboard with the name "TJ's Repair Shop" painted on it. This gave light to why there were so many tools and receipts strewn across the right side of the garage. Sifting my feet through the rubble, I covered the rest of the interior. Heading home, a valid lesson entered my mind. Never turn on any old switches when inside an abandoned location—one never knows, it may create an electrical fire.

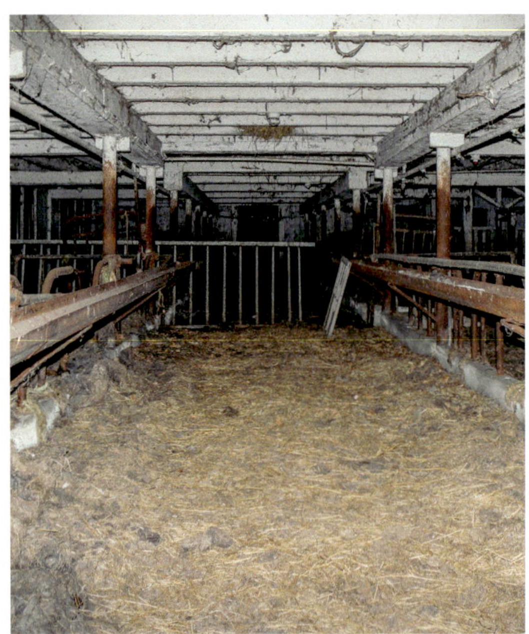

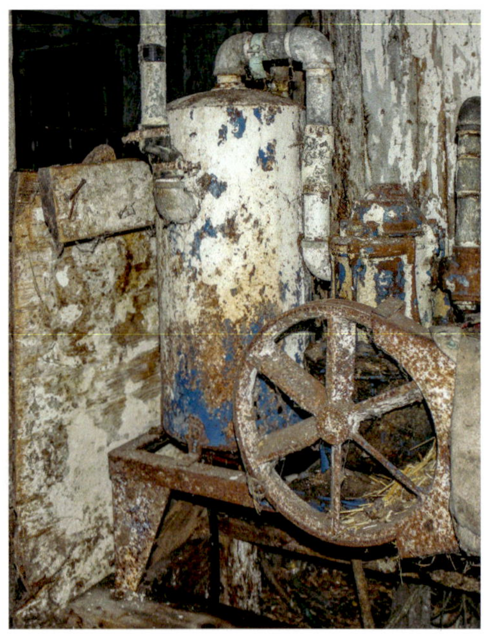

Above left: A view down the central aisle of the barns first floor, now blanketed in mold and old hay—once a home for many animals.

Above right: Sitting next to a ladder to the second floor lies a deceased industrial machine, encrusted with rust and lead paint.

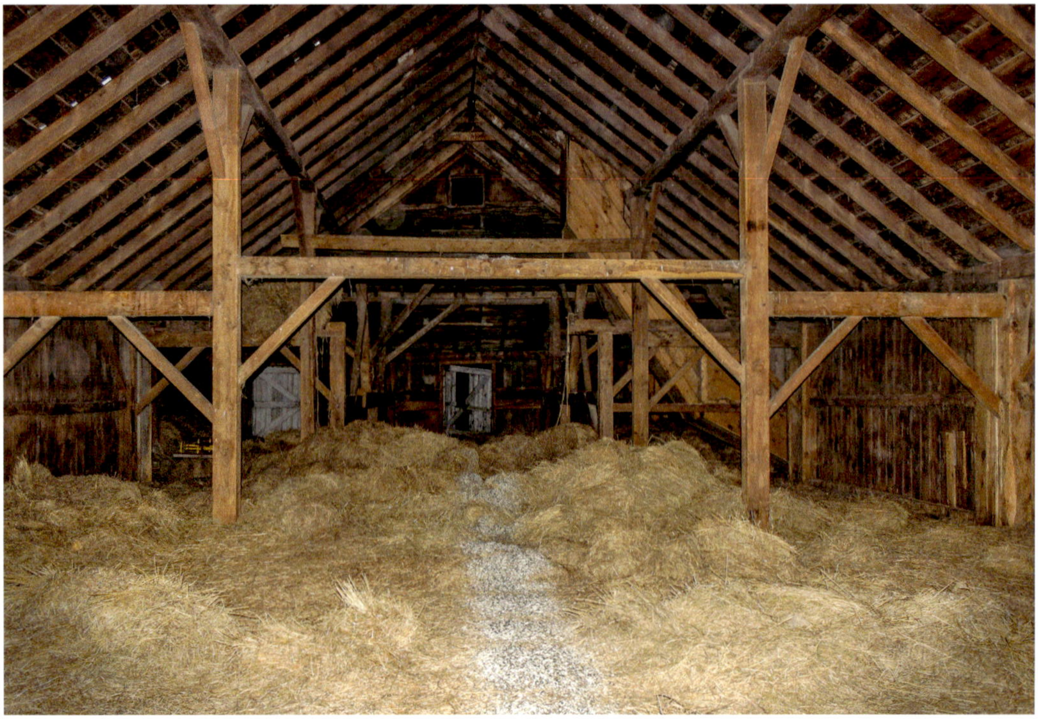

On the second floor, bird droppings line the middle of the hay soiled floor.

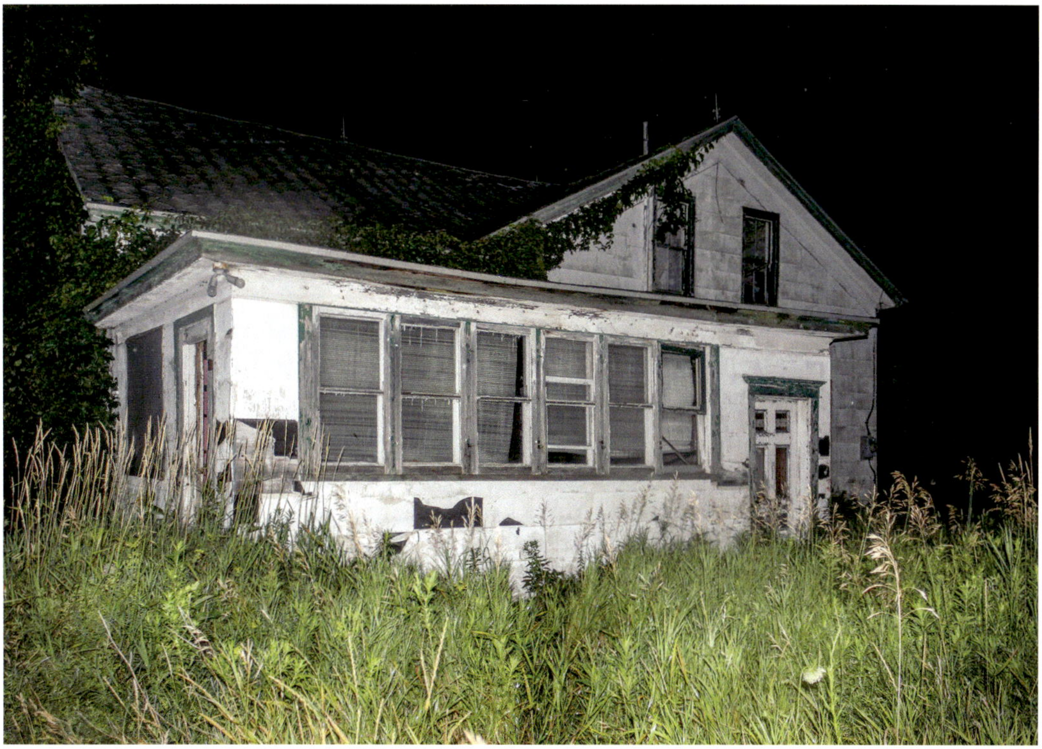

The house waits quietly in the dark marsh.

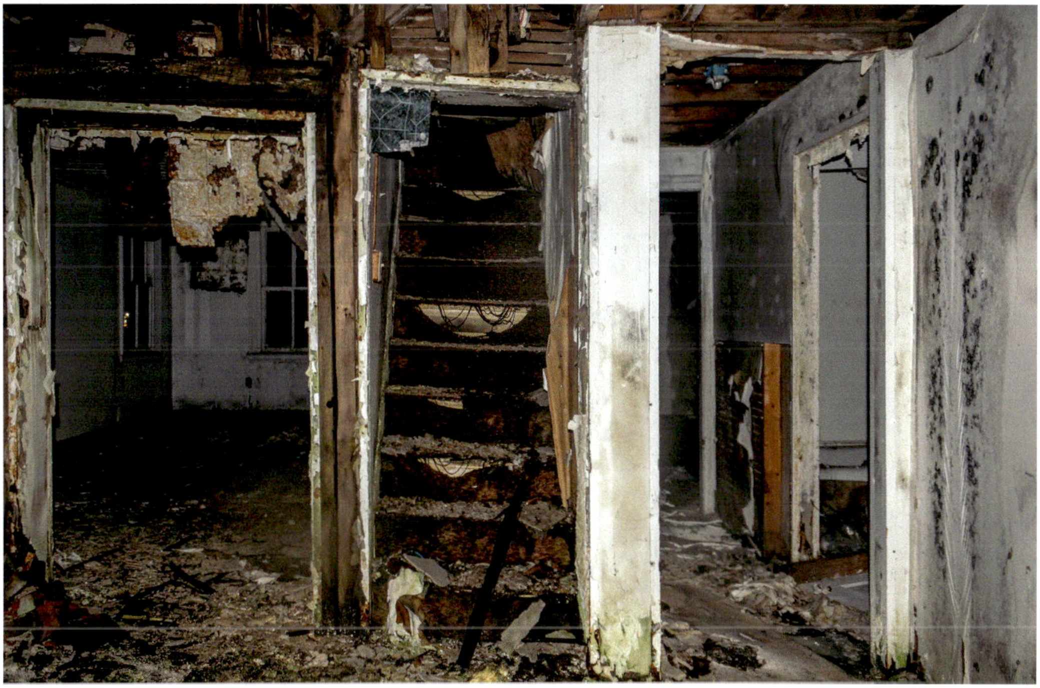

Obscene amounts of mold, a by-product from extreme water damage, deem this house detrimental to any explorer without a particle mask.

14

THE BLACK RIVER

I accidentally discovered these two locations while fishing on the Black River in Watertown, New York. I discovered the first location while making my way up the shore for a better cast. I recognized, from previous fishing trips, the multiple brick arches that protruded along the shore. Having to crouch under a few branches and brush, I found an opening inside the old brick structure. It had become completely reclaimed by nature. There wasn't much left of this structure, so its purpose remained a mystery to me. As for the second location, I had heard that Watertown was built over an expansive network of caves. I ventured into the neighboring woods in search of an entrance in the middle of the night. Luckily, I was able to gain access by crawling through a narrow hole, about three-and-a-half feet wide. The cavern was collapsed. Underwhelmed by the experience, I started making my way back to my car, but got lost in the process. Trying not to panic, I diverted my mind back to a story that I had heard about some train cars that were abandoned along the edge of the Black River. By an incredible coincidence, I turned on my flashlight and discovered two train cars, succumbed to rusting in the seclusion of the woods. This awesome find, paired with the opportunity of having gone fishing with my camera, made this trip extremely worthwhile. I inspected the forgotten train cars, then made my way back to the road and eventually found my car.

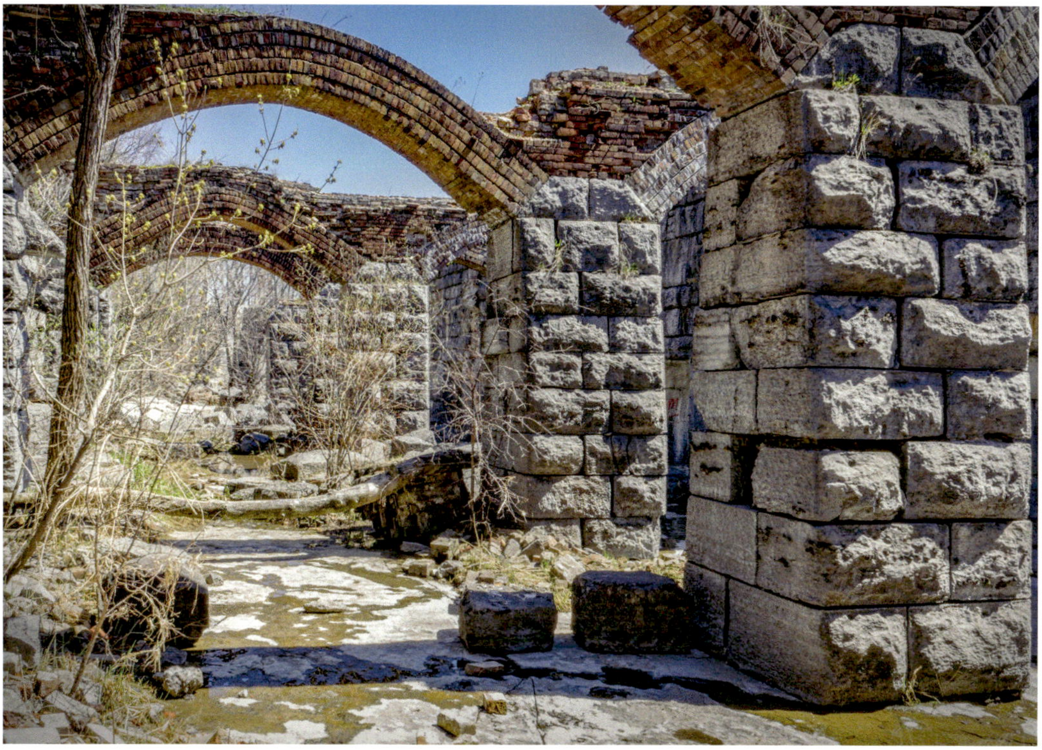

A view from where I had entered the large brick structure.

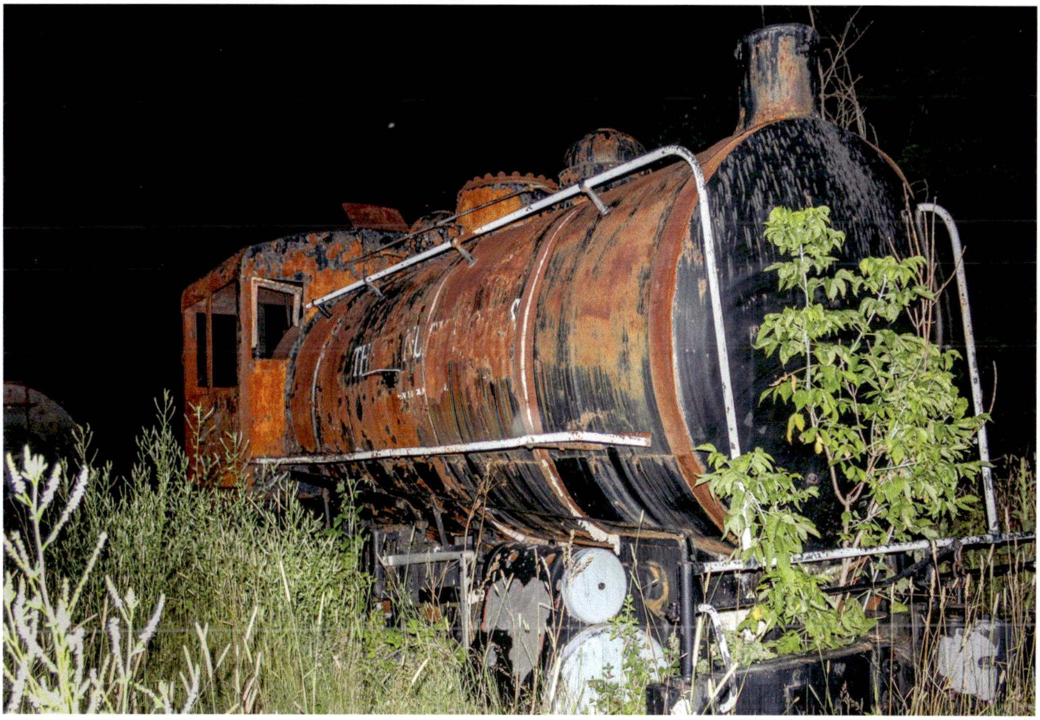

One of the train cars, caked in rust, courtesy of the harsh elements of Northern New York.

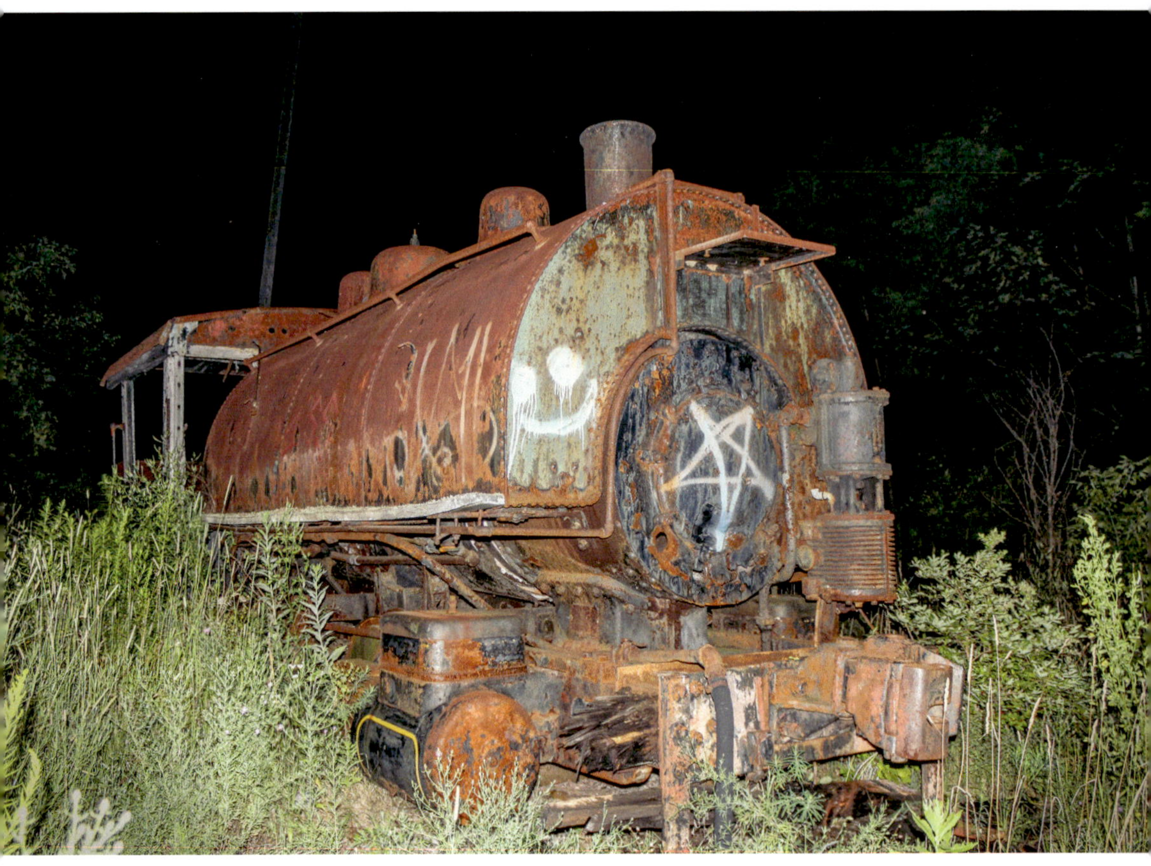

The second train car, far from pristine and decorated in graffiti.